THE PLAN

THE PLAN

KAREN GEISLER

REDEMPTION PRESS

Published by Redemption Press, PO Box 427, Enumclaw, WA 98022

Toll Free (844) 2REDEEM (273-3336)

Redemption Press is honored to present this title in partnership with the author. The views expressed or implied in this work are those of the author. Redemption Press provides our imprint seal representing design excellence, creative content and high quality production.

While this story is a fanciful tale of a boy who lived in Jesus's time, it also follows real events. The story of God's love throughout the ages, of his love for mankind and his moving through Jewish history to accomplish his plan, is clearly told in Scripture. Where appropriate, I have followed the biblical accounts closely, though I have paraphrased actual speech from Scripture.

The Holy Bible, King James Version. Public domain.

The Holy Bible, New International Version®, NIV® Copyright ©1973, 1978, 1984, 2011 by Biblica, Inc.® Used by permission. All rights reserved worldwide.

New Revised Standard Version Bible, copyright © 1989 the Division of Christian Education of the National Council of the Churches of Christ in the United States of America. Used by permission. All rights reserved.

ISBN 13: 978-1-68314-731-2
ePub ISBN: 978-1-68314-732-9
Kindle ISBN: 978-1-68314-733-6
Library of Congress Catalog Card Number: 2018964834

CONTENTS

PREFACE

I was born into a Christian family, and my faith was grounded through years of biblical teachings, both at home and in the church. I knew in my head and my heart what it meant to be a Christian. I had no doubt that Jesus died for me, yet deep down, I didn't fully appreciate what Jesus did for me on that cross. It was hard for me to relate to it.

The best way to explain my lack of appreciation is to compare my faith to being born with the proverbial silver spoon in my mouth. I'm rich, but I don't know anything but rich, so I don't appreciate it.

For years, this troubled me. I often asked God to help me understand and appreciate what Jesus did. It was in writing this book that I finally experienced that understanding through the eyes and heart of a child. I pray God touches your heart, as he did mine, through this book.

CHAPTER 1

GETTING ANSWERS

I kick every rock in sight as I walk down the dirt path. I'm annoyed and upset, but not at the rocks. I want to go with Dad and Grandpa to find the man named Jesus, but I'm not allowed. I'm not old enough.

I'm old enough to watch the sheep by myself, but I'm not old enough to be called Abraham. I'm old enough to hear grown-ups talk about important things, but not old enough to go find Jesus. It might be dangerous. I am old enough.

I kick another rock, but this time it catches my toe and it hurts. I stop to rub my foot. Jesus is all anybody talks about anymore. If someone makes a trip to Bethlehem or Jerusalem, we all get together to hear their stories.

Jesus heals people who can't walk or are blind. We even heard a story about how he fed five thousand people with just five loaves of bread and two fish! Every time one of our neighbors makes a trip, they come back with more stories about Jesus. The more I hear, the more I want to meet him. Maybe he could even heal Mom. She's been sick for a long time.

Grandpa is convinced that Jesus is the baby he saw in Bethlehem thirty years ago. Back then, nobody believed that Grandpa and his friends had seen angels in the sky or that the angels had told them to go see a baby who was born in a barn.

I try to imagine what it was like that night—sitting in the dark, watching the sheep . . . and then the sky lit up.

Grandpa says he saw angels as bright as the sun, flying back and forth in the sky. One of them said, "I have good news for everybody. A baby has been born who will save the world." And then the angel told Grandpa he'd find the baby in a barn at Bethlehem.

I stare at the sky, but no matter how hard I try, I just can't imagine it being filled with angels.

So Grandpa and his friends went to Bethlehem and found that baby, just like the angel said. Nobody knows what happened to the baby or that family, but Grandpa tells that story over and over to anyone who'll listen. Now, after hearing all the stories about Jesus, Grandpa's certain Jesus is the baby he saw thirty years ago.

Still rubbing my toe, I notice the sheep have made their turn and are heading to the pasture. Dad and Grandpa are saying goodbye to my brother, Adam. I run to catch up with them, hoping I can make them change their minds and let me go with them. I'm out of breath when I get there, but I still ask, "Dad, can I please go with you? Please?"

Dad doesn't get mad. He just says, "Son, we don't know what we'll run into. There are a lot of people on the roads traveling to see and hear Jesus, but there are bad people out there too. It could be dangerous for all of us. I'll feel a lot better with you at home helping your brother with the sheep."

Grandpa gives my hair a toss with his big, wrinkled hand. "Your dad is right."

When Dad makes up his mind, there's no changing it. I know he isn't trying to be mean. I have the best dad in the world—he just doesn't understand how much I want to go.

Adam sees how upset I am, so he wraps his arm around my shoulders. "Come on, Abe. You'll get your chance to see Jesus one of these days. It just isn't going to be today."

By now almost all the sheep are in front of us. They know their way to the pasture, and they aren't waiting for us. Dad and Grandpa walk down the path that takes them to the main road. I've been on that main road several times to go to Bethlehem. But the few trips I took with Dad to Jerusalem, I was younger. And we didn't stay very long. Adam is right—one day I will go to Jerusalem and see Jesus.

It takes almost all day to get the sheep to the grazing pasture. The sheep move slowly. We find a place to sleep for the night. I don't feel like talking, so I offer, "I'm going to go find wood for our fire."

"Sure, okay," Adam agrees, and I walk over to the trees and bushes to look for firewood.

My head is spinning with questions. I wonder how Jesus does his miracles. Why is he so special? How does he heal people? Is he the baby Grandpa saw in the manger? Grandpa says that baby was the Messiah. Could Jesus be the Messiah? The one we've been waiting for—the one who will save us from our enemies? I would do almost anything to see Jesus and find the answers to all my questions.

I shift the sticks and branches I'm holding to make room for more. If I catch up with Dad and Grandpa on the road, they won't make me go back by myself. I can tell Adam I'm going home. He won't care, especially since our neighbor by the creek is staying with Mom while we're all gone. It would mean she could go home.

The sun is pretty low now. I don't know if I can find my way in the dark, but if I can find that path that leads down to the main road, I should be okay. Then, when I get to the main road, I just have to go right instead of left. After that, I'm sure I can catch up to them.

It's now or never. I go back to Adam and dump the wood on the ground. "Adam, do you care if I don't stay out here with you? I want to go home." I give him the saddest face I can.

He looks out at the setting sun. "It's going to be night soon. Are you sure you can find your way home in the dark?"

I know I shouldn't do this, but I can't help myself. "I'll just run and get home before it gets dark."

Adam shrugs his shoulders. "Okay, just be careful. If you don't make it home before it gets dark, stop for the night. It's easy to get lost in these hills. I've gotten lost more than once out here."

"Okay!" I'm already running down the hill.

"Promise me you'll stop for the night if it gets dark before you get home!" Adam yells.

"I promise!" I holler back.

"Don't get lost!" Adam hollers again.

I run as fast as I can. If I don't find the path that leads to the main road in time, my plan won't work. Then I'll never get to see Jesus.

I'm running toward the setting sun, which reminds me how little time I have before it gets dark. I run down one slope and up another hill. My lungs start to burn a little, but I can't stop. The sun is almost down. I can see only a tiny edge of it on the horizon.

The sun disappears, but I keep my eyes on the spot where I saw it last and keep running in that direction. Pretty soon, I can't see where I'm going anymore. I don't want to stop, but I do. I bend over with my hands on my knees and gasp for all the air I can get. I'm so mad at myself. I drop to the ground and pull my knees up close to my chest.

I look out at the dark, then press my head against my knees. I'll never see Jesus now. I start crying, and I can't stop. I cry because Dad and Grandpa left me home. I cry because I'll never get the answers to all my questions. I cry because I'm so close, but my plan didn't work.

I wipe my eyes and nose on my sleeve and look around. Night noises are all around me. Now I'm scared. Maybe Dad was right about me being too young. Adam wouldn't cry like I am, and he sure wouldn't feel scared. I wouldn't be scared if I had a fire. But I'm too scared to go look for wood in the dark.

Maybe if I lie flat on my back, the animals won't see me. I stretch out and stare up at the stars. That makes me think about Grandpa again. I wonder what it was like to see those angels. I wish an angel would come and answer my questions about Jesus. There are so many stars in the sky, but one catches my eye. It's moving! I think it's getting brighter.

I sit up and watch it get bigger and bigger. My heart is pounding. Suddenly, the star bursts open, and I see an angel. He floats down and sits right next to me. I'm so scared I can't breathe. It was pitch black a second ago, but now it feels like daylight. He looks young like me, and he's wearing normal clothes. He doesn't have wings like I thought he would. Maybe they're under his clothes. I'm not sure. I have to shield my eyes from the bright light.

He throws his arms up. "Sorry. I forgot how bright I am." The brightness dims to a soft glow. "Hi, my name is Zagzagel, but you can call me Zag."

I'm breathing better now, but I can't talk. I can only stare.

"Don't be scared," Zag says. "You've heard of angels before, haven't you?"

Still staring, I mutter, "Yes." I'm sure he can see how scared I am.

"Well, I'm your angel." He stands up and waves his hand in the air like he's taking a bow. "I'm assigned to you, and it's my job to watch out for you. So you don't have to be afraid of me."

All of a sudden, it hits me like a big rock. I got what I wished for! I bet this angel can tell me about Jesus.

Zag doesn't skip a beat. "So you want to hear all about Jesus, huh?"

That stuns me enough to snap me out of my fear. I forget I'm talking to an angel when I say, "Hey! That was in my thoughts. I didn't say it out loud. How did you know?"

"Thoughts, words—they're all the same to me. And yes, that baby your grandpa saw in the barn was Jesus."

Wow, that trip with Dad and Grandpa isn't so important anymore. This is way better. My questions spill out. "Can you tell me where he grew up? Why is he here? Why is he so special? Did he come to save us from our enemies?"

Zag puts his hand up to stop the questions. "Look," he says, "Jesus being born in that barn is almost the end of the story. The story really began a few thousand years ago. Want to hear it?"

I can hardly hold back my excitement. "Yes!"

Zag rubs his chin. "Well, I could show you instead of tell you. That is, if you want to take a little trip with me."

I scramble to my feet. "You bet!"

Zag holds out his hand. "Okay, hold my hand and don't let go. We'll be going back in time. If you let go, I'm not sure I'll be able to find you."

I don't know what "going back in time" means. Is it like a vision, or will we actually go back days or years? Could I really get lost? I put my hands behind my back and cautiously ask, "What do you mean, go back in time?"

"You and I will go back and see the story instead of me telling you the story."

"But what if I get stuck back there and can't get home?"

Zag laughs. "You'll feel, hear, and see everything that's going on, but I promise I won't leave you behind. It's my job to take care of you, remember?"

I decide I can trust him. "Okay."

"Great! So you want to know why Jesus came and why he has to save you from your enemies?" Zag folds his arms across his chest and shakes his head back and forth. "Those are some big questions. We'll have to go back to the beginning of time to answer them, all the way back to Adam and Eve in the garden of Eden. You ready?"

I am so anxious to get the answers to all my questions about Jesus that I say yes without giving it a second thought.

Zag takes my hand. "Hold on tight," he says. "I don't want to lose you."

What does he mean, lose me?

He looks at me and laughs. "Just kidding. I won't lose you, I promise. But you do need to hold on tight, because going back in time can be a rough ride."

In that moment, we float upward, and everything spins. I hear Zag say, "Here we go. Hold on!"

* * *

It's so dark, I can hardly see anything. Every once in a while I think I see something, but everything is spinning so fast, I can't tell what it is. I feel sick, and I close my eyes as tight as I can.

I hear creepy noises, almost like hundreds of voices off in the distance, but I can't tell what they're saying. The wind is strong, and I start to flap back and forth through the air like a rag. I feel like I'm going to get pulled away from Zag. I pull my body forward as hard as I can until I can reach out and grab Zag with both hands. It's hard to breathe, so I press my face into my shoulder.

Now it's getting cold. I'm so cold, I'm freezing. My hands are numb. I don't know if it's from the cold or from holding on to Zag so tight.

I want to stop because I can't hold on any longer. My hands are slipping, and I start to scream—and then everything starts to slow down.

My body isn't being pulled away from Zag anymore. I drop one hand to my side and take a deep breath. I try to shake the numbness out of my hands as I open my eyes.

The earth is still turning way below us. Finally it stops. The earth is so thick with green trees and plants, I can't see the ground.

"That's the garden of Eden," Zag says.

I can't believe what I'm seeing. The garden is huge, but beyond it, the ground is brown in every direction as far as I can see, except one. There I see water—more water than I've ever seen in my life. It's a deep, dark, greenish blue with waves that pound against the edge of the land.

Six black-and-white fish, the size of a house, jump out of the water. I look at Zag. My expression must be pretty funny, because he grins as he says, "Yeah, God created those fish. They're called whales."

The sun here is hot, but I can see the other side of the earth too, and it's dark. I stretch to look around at the dark side, and I can see the moon and stars. I was just lying under those stars a minute ago, or maybe years ago? Did this just happen? Am I dreaming?

Zag gives my hand a squeeze.

I can feel it, so I guess I'm awake.

He says, "Before we land, I have to tell you how this all started. First, you need to know that God has a lot of love to give. He has more love than anyone can imagine. Nobody loves us as much as God does."

I think about that. I wonder what the world would be like if everybody loved like God does.

"God loved the people he created. He wanted to walk and talk with them. All they had to do was love him back."

"What do you mean?" I ask. "How can anyone walk and talk with God?"

Zag smiles. "One day you will, Abe. That's all part of God's plan."

"God has a plan?"

Zag ignores my question but says, "God created all of this to be your home."

But the earth has always been here, I think. I've never thought much about God creating it or why he created it.

"The earth is brand new. The trees and bushes haven't had a chance to grow yet. That's why God created this garden for Adam and Eve."

I still can't believe what I'm seeing. I really did go back in time. Dad and Grandpa will never believe this.

"Want to go see it?"

"Yes!"

We move closer to the earth, and I see rivers winding through the thick forests. I see animals standing at the edge of a river, drinking water. Birds are everywhere, soaring through the sky, gliding just above the water.

Suddenly, I see two people walking around under the green blanket of trees. "Is that Adam and Eve?"

With a look of love and admiration, Zag answers. "Yes, that's Adam and Eve. God takes great joy in them." Zag gets a faraway look on his face.

I wonder what he's thinking. "Will it be awkward if they see us?"

Zag snaps out of his thoughts. "You won't even be close to them. Besides that, nobody can see you. Not even the animals can see you. When you're in the garden, you'll be able to see, touch, smell, and even taste things. You'll be able to see whatever you want, but no one will see you. So don't be afraid to explore."

I'm starting to get excited.

As we get closer to the earth, Adam and Eve disappear.

Zag says, "God loves them so much, there isn't anything he wouldn't do for them. But they're going to sin, and that will change everything."

I know about sin—it's in the Torah. But why will things change when it happens? What will change? "But Zag," I protest, "the Law of Moses says if we sin, we just have to sacrifice an animal. Doesn't that work for Adam and Eve?"

Zag rubs his chin. "Let me see. How can I explain this?" Zag has that thinking-hard look again. "Okay, you know how hot you get when you stand in the sun in the summer?" he asks.

"Yes. My skin burns if I stand in the sun too long."

"And how does the sun feel when the sky is filled with clouds?"

"It's not hot, and my skin doesn't burn."

Zag holds out his left hand and says, "This is the sun. It's hot, and it burns." Then he holds out his right hand. "This is also the sun, but it's cool and won't burn. What's the difference?"

"The clouds?"

Zag claps his hands together. "Yes! And Adam and Eve's sin will create a barrier between you and God like the clouds that cover the sun."

"So sacrificing an animal doesn't fix that?"

"Not completely. When you sin, it's like the sun going behind a big, thick cloud. You sacrifice an animal to atone for your sin, and the sun comes out again, but it's still behind a thin layer of clouds. Got it?"

"So . . . no matter what, there will always be a barrier between us and God?"

"Yes. But God has a plan to fix that."

I nearly forget we're back in the beginning of time. We're about to land in the garden of Eden, but with every question Zag answers, I feel like it gives me another question to ask, like this one: "What do you mean, 'God has a plan'?"

"Let's just go into the garden. That might help answer some of your questions."

Our feet touch the ground. I look around, and it's beautiful. The bushes are full of black, blue, and red berries. It doesn't feel wrong to reach out and pick one. I taste it, and a sweet juice explodes in my mouth. I pick a handful of them. The trees all around me are full of fruit I've never seen before.

I don't see Zag anywhere, but it doesn't matter because I don't have a question in my head. Not one. I can feel the warmth of the sun, even though I'm in the shade. I feel peaceful. I've never felt like this before. There's so much love inside me, I feel like I love every person and every thing.

I think about God and how much he loves Adam and Eve. I can feel God here . . . which is strange, because I've never felt this before. There's a love for God growing inside of me. I think my heart is going to burst. I know God can see how much I love him.

I hear a noise behind me. I turn to see what it is, and the bushes are moving. A huge lion pokes his head out. He has long hair around his head that flows down to his knees. He makes a muffled roar, licks his lips, and comes right up to me.

I should be scared to death, but I'm not. The lion walks right past me. I put my hand on his back to feel his warm fur. As he walks away from me, I let my hand ride down his back. I catch his tail, and it glides through my fingers as he walks on. It all feels so natural and perfect.

I know I have to go home eventually, but I don't want to leave. I'm alone, but I don't feel alone. I feel happy and . . . so much love. I don't feel afraid of anything. I sit down on the ground and lean against a tree. I look up at the birds in the trees and listen to them chirping and singing. I savor the sweet taste of the last berry I picked.

I stand up to get more berries, and suddenly everything changes. I can't see it, but something bad is happening. It almost feels like part of me is being pulled out from the inside. I don't understand it. I panic and look for Zag but don't see him. I start running through the trees and hollering. "Zag! Where are you?" I trip and fall into some thick bushes.

I'm pushing through the bushes when I see that lion again. He's different too. I gasp so hard I start to choke. I drop down into the bushes and watch him through the leaves. He's looking right at me and growling. I'm so scared, I can feel my heart pounding. The lion crouches to leap at me.

I squeeze my eyes shut. "Please, God," I plead. "Help me! I want to go home."

I curl up as tight as I can under the bush and don't move. I don't even breathe. I hear a grunt as the lion leaps. His feet hit the bush. I wait for his pounce, but nothing. I peek out to see where he is, and he's running away from me, chasing a goat.

The lion is gone, but I'm still so scared I don't want to come out of the bush. I don't even want to holler for Zag in case another wild animal hears me. My whole body is shaking. I can't even pretend to feel that love I felt before. All I feel is fear, and I want to get out of here.

And just like that, Zag is standing next to the bush, looking down at me.

"Sorry about that. I knew nothing bad was going to happen to you. But then, you didn't know that, did you?"

I climb out of the bush and brush off the leaves and dirt. I'm so happy to see him. "What happened?"

Zag's voice is sad and quiet. "Adam and Eve sinned," he says.

Zag keeps his head down and doesn't say another word. That's good, because it gives me time to think about what he said. I remember the moment when I felt everything change. That must have been the moment when they sinned.

Zag interrupts my thoughts. "Abe, what you felt first was what life was like without sin. There was no barrier between you and God. What you felt when everything changed was that barrier going up between you and God. And yeah, sin brings fear and a lot of other stuff."

"But you said God has a plan to get rid of that barrier. What's his plan?"

"He's going to send his Son to fix it."

"Is that Jesus?"

"Yes."

"But I don't understand," I protest. "Why doesn't God send Jesus right away? Why does he wait thousands of years to send Jesus?"

Zag gives his head a small shake and smiles. "It's not that easy. Jesus will have to be born like you were. Who'll be his mother? It can't be just anybody. She must be someone devoted to God. Not just her, but her family and her neighbors and her nation. We don't want Jesus to grow up and find that nobody believes in God, right?"

I nod because it makes sense.

"God needs a nation of people who will trust him for anything. That will take some time. About fifteen hundred years from now, nobody will even remember who God is anymore."

I interrupt and say, "Except for Noah! Grandpa told me that story."

"Good. Then we can skip that part."

I'd like to see the ark and the flood, but Zag doesn't give me a chance to ask.

"After the flood, it doesn't take long for people to forget about God again. So God decides to start with one man. About four hundred years go by after the flood. Then God finds a man who will be the father of this nation. Want to go see?"

I start to panic because time travel is scary.

Zag sees my fear. "Look, going forward in time is nothing like going backward. The earth turns, but we don't. Come on, hold my hand."

I have no choice—I have to take Zag's hand. We float upward just as the earth starts to turn. Again, I can't believe what I'm seeing.

Zag is still talking. "Hey, you're named after this guy. His name is Abram, but God changes his name to Abraham."

I thought about my nickname. "I wish my dad would call me Abraham. He says he'll call me that when I'm older. It's not that I don't like being called Abe, but . . . it just seems like I'll never be old enough for anything."

Zag smiles. "He will, you'll see. Things will be different soon."

The earth stops turning.

"We aren't going to land," Zag says. "We're just going to stop long enough to see Abraham."

There's a caravan of people traveling below us. I can see a tall, older man with long white hair. He's walking with a stick that's taller than he is.

I take a guess. "So that's him?"

"That's him. That's Abraham. He just packed up his things and his family and headed west because God asked him to."

We watch as the caravan moves steadily along.

Zag says, "I know God promised to bless the world through Abraham if he moved. But still, you have to admit, Abraham had to really trust God to make that move."

I can tell Zag is proud of Abraham. I'm sure God is too. I ask again, "So why can't God send Jesus now?"

"Abraham's faith isn't strong enough yet," Zag answers. "God has to teach Abraham that he can trust God no matter what. Then Abraham has to teach his son to trust God, and his grandchildren."

We watch a little longer, and Zag says, "God waited almost two thousand years for Abraham. He's not going to send Jesus until the time is right. But you have to agree, this is a great start."

"Yeah."

Zag squeezes my hand. "Time to move on," he says.

The earth begins to turn.

CHAPTER 2

LIVING THE STORIES

I'm so absorbed with watching the earth turn, I don't realize Zag is deep in thought. He looks sad. I don't know what to say, so I ask, "Where are we going next?" He doesn't hear me, so I bump his shoulder with mine to get his attention. "You okay?"

I can tell he's not, but he says, "Yeah. We're going to see Abraham's great-great-grandchildren." Something is definitely bothering him. He changes the subject. "Do you know who Jacob is?"

"Yeah, I remember him from Grandpa's stories. He's Abraham's grandson. God changes his name to Israel." Thinking about Grandpa's stories makes me think about Uncle Jacob. "My uncle makes fun of Grandpa for telling too many stories. I haven't seen Uncle Jacob for a long time because he moved to Jerusalem."

That seems to make Zag even sadder, so I ask again, "I know something is wrong. What's the matter?"

Zag tries to shake free from whatever it is. "It's really great your grandpa tells you stories about the Hebrew people," he says. "But what you're going to see next isn't a happy story. It's a sad time in their history. I'm sure your grandpa has told you this story before, but it's one thing to hear it and another thing to live it."

I look at Zag and wonder where we're going next.

"A famine forces Abraham's grandson, Israel, to move to Egypt," Zag continues. "Israel moved his whole family of sixty-six there. The Egyptians call them Hebrews because they're from the city of Hebron."

I remember Grandpa telling me about our people being called Hebrews. Now we're called Jewish people because we're from Judah.

"Abraham's great-grandson, Joseph, is already in Egypt, where the only person more powerful than he is, is the Pharaoh. Thanks to Joseph, the Hebrews get treated really well. They survive a seven-year famine. Life is so good for them that they decide to stay in Egypt.

"It takes less than a hundred years for this family to grow into a small nation. Joseph isn't alive anymore, and the new Pharaoh is afraid the Hebrews will take control. To make sure they don't, he turns them into slaves."

I'm getting excited, because I think we're going to Egypt.

"Your grandpa tells you stories. The grandpas who survive this slavery will tell stories to their grandchildren too. The stories will give them hope and help them keep their faith in God. Hope and faith are all they have. You ready to see more?"

I'm afraid something bad will happen like in the garden of Eden with that lion. I shiver just thinking about it. But good or bad, I really do want to see this. I nod my head. "Yes."

"Just remember, nobody can see you. You can walk around and look, but you might get bumped if you get too close to someone. I want you to take your time and see it all. This is a great example of the Hebrew people keeping their faith, no matter what."

Before I know it, my feet are on the ground. I'm standing next to mounds of straw. It feels like a safe place to stay for the moment. I look around for Zag but don't see him. I'm not even moving, and the sweat is rolling down my face from the blistering heat.

* * *

This is such a busy place. All around me are slaves. I've never seen so many people! Men, women, old people, even kids, and they're all working hard in this hot sun. I don't have words for what I'm seeing. It's way worse than what Grandpa said. It just isn't right.

Way out in the distance, I see a huge stone building. I'm not paying attention, and I almost fall backward when water splashes on my feet. A slave has passed by with a bucket of water and spilled it on me. I'm so hot that it makes me thirsty.

I watch other slaves carrying buckets of water. The buckets must be heavy, because the people walk about ten steps and put them down. Then they pick them up with their other hand. They give a drink to anyone who calls out for water. I look around to see where they're getting the water from.

Not too far away I see a well. A slave is there, filling buckets and lining them up around the well. Nearby, several soldiers are relaxing under the shade of a great big canvas, drinking water and being fanned by more slaves. I'm not sure if it's safe to go over there. The soldiers are one thing, but between me and that well, there's a lot of traffic too. I don't want to bump into anyone.

I'm too thirsty not to try, so I step out from my safe place and start walking. I zigzag back and forth around slaves. They are pushing carts full of sand and wagons full of hay. Some are driving horses, pulling flat wooden sleds that are heaped with bricks. I pass a few more slaves who are carrying a platform with a person on top of it. Why doesn't that person just walk?

I'm so busy looking around that I don't see the broken brick on the ground. My foot catches it, and I fall right in front of a group of slaves walking past me. Some of them trip over me, and right away, I hear this loud, cracking sound. I look up fast enough to see a whip coming down at me.

I put my arms around my head and roll into a ball. The whip hits its target—the slave next to me. I scramble to my feet as fast as I can and run. I'm bumping into people who can't see me, but I don't care. I must get away from that whip. I run until I can't hear it anymore.

I start to slow down, but then I hear the crack of another whip. There are soldiers everywhere! I stop at the top of a muddy slope that feels like a safe place. The whip I hear is coming from someplace else. There's a pit filled with straw and mud . . . and slaves. The slaves are filling buckets with the straw-and-mud mixture. Then they lift the buckets up to other slaves who dump them into a push cart.

One of them isn't working fast enough. The soldier hits him with a whip. Then he yells, "Faster, slave, or you'll taste my whip again!"

This place is horrible. I wrap my arms around myself but get no comfort from it. I have to stop watching. I start to walk away, looking back at that slave who is still bent over and bleeding in that muddy pit. And then I slip and feel myself falling.

It's so muddy that I can't stop myself from sliding down a slope toward a pit. I dig my heels into the ground, but it's all mud and I keep sliding. I land with a splash in the deep, slimy pit. I slam into two slaves, and they both fall. I look up, afraid we're going to be whipped, but the soldier is waving at someone up top. He didn't see us fall.

Ten slaves are in this pit, stomping in the mud. I push my way to the wall of the pit as fast as I can to get out of their way. I look for a way to climb out, but it looks hopeless. Then, without warning, all ten slaves start pushing to get space against the wall.

Still trying to avoid being bumped by the slaves, I crawl through the mud to the middle of the pit. The slaves are looking up. I look up too, just in time to see mounds of straw falling on top of me.

The straw is heavy and dusty, and it knocks me down. I can't breathe. I'm choking and coughing. I try to cover my mouth and nose with my sleeve, but it's full of mud. Finally I see light above, and I fight to reach for it. Ahh, I can breathe again.

The straw starts falling away from me. It's being pulled down into the mud from the edges. The slaves have moved back into the pit, and they're stomping the new straw into the mud. I move back to the wall to get out of their way. I have to get out of here.

My shoulders are level with the top edge of the slippery mud pit. I stretch my arms as far as I can and try to pull myself out. There's nothing to hold on to but mud. Then I realize it doesn't matter anyway—the weight of the mud on me is more than I can pull out. I'll have to wait and hopefully get out when the slaves do. I lean back against the wall and watch them.

I try to imagine how they feel. Five are women, probably my mom's age. I would hate for my mom to be stuck in a mud pit for even one day. Four are kids—three girls and one boy. I think they're my age. I feel guilty for being mad that Dad wouldn't take me with him. I'm sure these kids would love to spend a day in the pasture with sheep.

The tenth slave is a very old woman who can hardly lift her feet in the mud. The slaves talk to each other in low voices, I guess so the guard doesn't hear them. They keep the old woman between them to shield her from that whip.

I don't think I could keep my faith in God if I had to live like this. I would wonder every day why God doesn't come and save me. I watch these slaves. They are covered in mud. They look just like me, but beneath that mud, I can see they are tired and sad.

I don't want to think of them as just slaves in a story anymore. These are real people. Now I know why Zag was looking so sad.

Suddenly, they all push their way to the walls again. This time, I know what's coming, and I bend over and make an air pocket to breathe. The straw falls, and my air pocket fills up with straw dust. I hold my breath for as long as I can and wait. When I can't hold my breath any longer, I stand up, push the hay away, and take as deep a breath as I can handle. It's still dusty.

It's getting harder for the workers to pull their feet up from the thick, heavy mud. They can't slow down or stop because they'll get that whip. The mud is so thick now that I have to keep my feet moving so I don't get stuck. I can almost stand on top of it without sinking.

The soldier motions for someone, and I panic, thinking they're bringing more straw. But instead, I see a cart with men carrying buckets heading our way. I know what that means, and so do the women. They stand up on the mud and pull themselves out of the pit. Then they reach down to pull out the kids.

I have to get out of this pit before they start scooping out the mud. I crawl over to some dried mud on the other side of the pit and stand up. I bend over the edge and roll myself out of the pit. I feel so heavy with this mud on me, it's hard to stand up. I scrape as much off as I can, but I'm still extremely dirty.

I remember the well and decide to try again to get there. I must wash off this mud, and I really need a drink. I can't see the well from where I am, but I can see that big stone building. The well was in that direction, so I head over that way.

I walk past pit after pit of mud, and I'm careful not to fall into another one. I come to an area where they're dumping the mud mixture into molds to make bricks. I stop to watch. We have sand and straw at home. Maybe we can make bricks to build things. A loud crack of a whip rings in my ears, and it scares me so much that I run. I run until I'm too hot and tired to run anymore.

I guess I missed the well, because suddenly I'm at the stone building. It's even bigger and taller than I thought it was. I have to bend my head all the way back to see the top of it. Hundreds of Hebrew men are working on the building. Some are on tall ladders, pounding away at the stone with hammers. Some are dangling from ropes, chiseling on the rock to make shapes.

I can see tall poles inside the building connected to poles on the outside of the building. That tall pole frame is holding the weight of a huge stone dangling from a lot of ropes. Each rope has a guard holding a different-colored flag. I think each rope must pull the stone in a different direction. People are shouting orders. Hundreds of Hebrews are pulling on those ropes as hard as they can. Everyone looks tense. The soldiers with whips are there, making sure each rope is pulled at the right time.

Someone behind me keeps yelling "Pull, pull!" I walk over to where the sound is coming from. Hundreds more Hebrew men are tied together by a few ropes in long rows. They're pulling the biggest stone

I've ever seen. It's so huge I can't believe they're even able to pull it. I didn't know stones that large existed. I wonder where they got it from.

I walk up alongside them. They look tired but are pulling as hard as they can. An old man gets my attention. He's older than Grandpa. He's hot, sweaty, and very tired. He stumbles, and without thinking, I jump to catch him. I don't get there in time. A whip cracks the air between us and it makes me fall backward. It just misses me, but the old man is curled up in a ball, and there's blood on his back. The soldier standing over him coils his whip, then kicks the old man. "Get up and pull!" he hollers.

I want to help the old man, but I know can't. I push with my feet to back away. I keep pushing away until I get to what feels like a safe place. I pull my knees up to my chest and wrap my arms around my legs. Holding myself as tight as I can, I close my eyes to shut it all out. These are my relatives. They don't deserve this. The Hebrews are God's chosen people, and the Egyptians are trying to destroy them.

A hand touches my shoulder, and my whole body shudders. I'm sure the soldier has seen me.

But it's Zag. "When life is hard," he says, "it's tough to have faith. But these people keep their faith day after day. Amazing, isn't it?"

I am so happy to see Zag. I jump up to give him a hug, but he holds both hands up and backs away. "Whoa, not so fast. You're full of mud."

I look at myself, and we both start to laugh. I needed that laugh.

"I know just what you need to get rid of that mud," he says. "You're going to love this."

I'm not sure anything will be good at this point, but I really want to get out of here, so I grab his hand and up we drift. As the earth turns, I ask, "Where are we going?"

"How would you like to see God part the Red Sea?" Zag grins at me.

I don't think I'll get into trouble there. I remember every detail Grandpa told in this story. The Hebrews march right through the middle of the Red Sea. As soon as they get to the other side, the water crashes in on the Egyptian soldiers. Yes, I'm sure I'll be safe there.

"I would love to see that," I answer.

* * *

The earth stops, and I see a huge, roaring pillar of fire swirling around just above the ground. It's blocking Pharaoh's army from chasing after the Hebrews. There's a wide, dry path through the sea. Tall walls of water are holding it back on either side. The sea is noisy and all stirred up. It's pounding at the walls, trying to fall back where it belongs.

Zag and I are still floating. I look back at the pillar of fire.

Before I can ask, Zag says, "That there is the very presence of God."

I know Zag has seen this before, but we both watch in awe. That whole pillar of fire is turning and rolling around in one spot. Roaring explosions of fire break loose all around it, shooting flames high into the sky above.

We watch, spellbound, for several minutes. Then Zag says, "We'd better get moving. The Hebrews are halfway through the sea."

When my feet hit the ground, I'm standing on the edge of the shore. I'm still staring at the pillar of fire thinking what a powerful God we have. How can I ever lose my faith in him?

The roaring of the water breaks my thoughts, and I turn to look at the sea. I step down onto the sea floor, and it's littered with shells.

I feel a light mist of water on my face, but the ground is dry. I walk farther into the seabed, right down the middle. The farther in I walk, the louder the roar of the water gets.

I walk over to the wall on my right. I hold my hand flat toward it, but I don't touch it. I want to touch it, but I'm afraid to. But if I don't, I know I'll always wish I did. I close my eyes and push my hand into the wall. It goes right into the water, and I pull it back quickly.

It doesn't seem to hurt anything. Cautiously, I put my hand back into the wall just a little, and then I start running. My hand skims along the wall, and the water splashes back at me. The mud in my clothes begins to wash away. Getting braver, I shove my arm in up to my shoulder, and water splashes all around me. This is more fun than I ever remember having. I am soaking wet. I don't think I have a spot of mud left on me.

I look down the center of the sea. The Hebrews are almost all the way across. I look behind me, and the pillar of fire is still there. But I remember Grandpa's story, and I know the pillar will lift and Pharaoh's soldiers will race down upon me. I look back at the Hebrews, and with absolute fear, I run.

I don't see the walls. I don't hear the roar. I don't feel the mist. I just keep running. I've almost caught up to the Hebrews, but I'm so out of breath, I have to stop. I bend over, put my hands on my knees, and gasp for air.

I lift my head up and watch as the last of the Hebrews climb the bank. I spin around, and the pillar of fire is gone. I can hear the Egyptians. I can hear their horses galloping and the soldiers shouting. They're coming. I scream above the roar of the water, "God, help me!"

I'm still gasping for air, but I run as hard as I can. I can hear them behind me. I'm so close to the other side, I can't stop. I reach the bank, but it's steep and full of big boulders. I start climbing, but I'm only halfway up when I hear the water moving behind me. I grab one of the big boulders and hold on to it as tightly as I can. I take a deep breath and shut my eyes just as the heavy water crashes down on me.

The force of the water pushes me against the boulder. I can't breathe. Now the water falls back into the sea, and it tries to pull me with it. I'm holding on to my boulder so tightly that my arms feel numb. The water rolls off me, and I gasp for air. Another wave rolls over me, but it's not as fierce. The sea is calming down.

It's almost as if the sea is glad to be back to its normal shape. I finally let go of the boulder and realize it's part of the bank. I roll over and lie on my back. My arms are aching, and I'm still trying to catch my breath. I can hear the sea, but otherwise, the air is still and quiet— so quiet it almost hurts my ears. There's a nation of Hebrews on the banks above me, but they aren't making a sound.

Then a soft voice breaks the silence—a woman, singing. I remember Grandpa saying Moses's sister, Miriam, sang a song. It has to be her I hear.

"I will sing to the Lord. He has triumphed gloriously. Horse and rider, he has thrown into the sea. The Lord is my strength and my might. He has become my salvation. This is my God, and I will praise him."

Tears slide down my wet face. I feel an explosion of faith inside of me. I have no doubt in my mind that God has a plan. And he chose my people to make that plan happen! I am so proud of them. They suffered so much and didn't lose their faith in God.

"That was really something, eh?"

I jump up so quickly, I almost fall down the bank. Zag sure has a way of getting my attention, but I'm glad to see him. Smiling, I say, "It sure was."

CHAPTER 3

THE PLAN HAS A PRICE

We're floating again, and the earth is turning. Zag says, "Do you need to see any more to understand why Jesus came?"

"Umm, yes. I mean, no. No, I don't need to see anything more, and yes, I do understand why Jesus came. And I really do believe God has a plan. I don't think anything can stop it."

"Good." Zag pauses, and I can tell he's thinking hard. Finally he says, "There's just one more thing I want you to see. You won't like it, but I think you've seen enough to trust God's plan, no matter what."

I don't know what to say. I can't imagine what could be worse than seeing the Hebrews as slaves in Egypt.

"Do you remember hearing any readings from the prophet Isaiah?"

"Yes. Isaiah is Grandpa's favorite prophet. Grandpa reads his writings to me all the time."

"Good. Our next stop is a visit with Isaiah."

The earth slows down. It's dark outside, but the moon is shining brightly. We land in the center of a city, in front of a building full of people.

"Here's where we're headed," Zag says. He opens the door, and we walk in. This time he doesn't disappear.

Four lamp stands light up the room enough for me to see about a hundred people here. An old man is seated at the front of the room. It must be Isaiah. He's bent over with his hands clasped in his lap. I can't hear what he's saying. Zag motions for me to get closer. Nobody can see me, so I walk right up next to Isaiah.

His skin is wrinkled and tan like leather. His hair is white as snow and hangs over his shoulders. He stops talking for a minute and shakes his head. He seems to be having a hard time saying what he wants to say. Everybody in the room, including me, waits for him to speak again.

In a quiet, tearful voice, he says, "It's our sins that rip and crush him . . . our sins! He takes the punishment that will make us whole. By his bruises, we will be healed."

Isaiah stops and takes a deep breath. After another few moments of silence, he shakes his head again. "We're all like sheep that have wandered off and gotten lost. We've all done our own thing, gone our own way." He pounds his clenched hands into his lap. He cries out, "God will pile all our sins, everything we've ever done wrong, on him . . . on him!"

His eyes are full of tears that begin rolling down his cheeks. His voice breaks as he says, "He'll be beaten and tortured. Like a lamb, he'll be taken to the slaughter."

Keeping his hands locked, he wipes his wet face with his sleeve. With a pleading look, he continues. "He won't say a word. Will anyone even know what's happening? He'll be beaten bloody for our sins. He'll die without even thinking about himself. They'll bury him in a rich man's grave. All this to someone who will have never hurt a soul or said one word that isn't true."

This is so sad. I can't figure out why Zag wants me to hear what Isaiah is saying. Then it hits me. It's Jesus he's talking about. My heart starts racing so fast I almost can't breathe. No! It can't be Jesus, because God wouldn't let Jesus be killed. God has a plan! If Jesus is killed, how can he save us?

I don't want to believe it. It can't be true. I gasp for air.

* * *

We're floating again. The earth is turning and Isaiah is way behind us, but I can't stop crying.

"That can't be true, Zag! It can't be Jesus! Tell me it isn't Jesus."

Zag is careful not to let go as he puts his arm around me. "Abe, I know you don't want anything to happen to Jesus. But you're thinking like a human thinks, not like God thinks. God loves Jesus more than anything, but that's what it's going to take. Jesus is the Messiah. Jesus is the only one who can pay the price for all the sin that has ever been committed.

"He'll even pay for all the sins that have yet to be committed by future generations. This is what Jesus is born to do." He hugs me. "Jesus knows what he has to do, and he's doing it out of pure love. Most people won't even realize what's happening when it happens. But this is God's plan to save the world. God isn't saving the world from its enemies. He's saving people from sin. Jesus is the perfect sacrifice."

I don't say anything. I can't. I know he's right. It all makes sense. But it's such a horrible plan. God can do anything! Why does Jesus have to die? Why can't God do some sort of amazing miracle and save Jesus? I don't understand. And I don't want to think about it anymore.

Zag takes his arm off my shoulder but forgets to take hold of my hand. I gasp when I start to drift away from him.

He grabs my hand and says, "Oops. Sorry about that."

It really scared me that I might get lost in time. Now all I can think about is holding Zag's hand as tightly as I can.

Zag bumps my shoulder with his. "Did you know Isaiah and King David both said the Savior will die?" Then, with a grin, he adds, "But they also said he will live again."

That confuses me even more. How can he live again?

"Maybe that will help you to trust God's plan"—Zag squeezes my hand—"no matter what happens."

I don't answer him because, deep down, I don't want to believe Jesus is going to die. My whole idea of life has changed so much since I started this adventure with Zag.

Zag nudges me again. "You ready to go see Jesus, Abe?"

Oh! I've been so worried about Jesus that I forgot I wanted to see him. It doesn't take me long to answer, "Yes!"

I'm staring at the earth turning.

"You want to know why I think it's the right time for Jesus to come?" Zag asks.

That's exactly what I've been wondering.

"Well, there are two people in Rome, Anthony and Octavian. They both want to rule Rome. That means war. They're fighting over many lands, including Judah. Before it's over, half the Jewish people will be kidnapped and forced to be slaves. They'll be property, like a cow or a sheep."

I shiver just thinking about slaves.

"And the farmers and people who own a business, if they don't pay their taxes, they're forced to sell their homes, land, and businesses for almost nothing."

That makes me think about Dad and Grandpa. They're always trying to figure out how to pay our taxes. Dad has a box he hides behind a stone in our fireplace that he keeps his money in. He marks off the weeks he has left before he has to pay his taxes. I feel bad whenever Dad pulls that box out, because it makes him worry.

Zag's still talking. "Most of Judah already struggles just to feed their families. They don't have money to see a doctor when they get sick. The few who are rich and own slaves don't do anything to help the poor."

That makes me think about Mom. She's been so sick. We all try to help her and make it easier for her. Dad wants her to see a doctor, but she says we can't afford to pay one. Mom insists it isn't anything a doctor can help with anyway. I think the people Zag is talking about are people like us.

"Octavian is the emperor of Rome now. He's declared Judah a nation and made Herod the king of Judah. He also assigned a man from Rome to be Judah's governor. That governor made Caiaphas the high priest. Nobody in Judah likes Rome telling them what to do. But they don't object, because they're afraid of losing their status as a nation."

Now I know he's talking about us. I remember Grandpa being mad when Caiaphas became the high priest.

Zag nods and continues. "When your grandpa was young, Herod built arenas, palaces, and theaters while people were starving. He even rebuilt the temple in Jerusalem."

I have to interrupt. "I know! But Grandpa says that Herod murdered a lot of people, especially his own family. And Herod had all those babies in Bethlehem killed. Grandpa was pretty sure Herod found and killed that baby he saw in the barn. He always wondered about that."

"Well, see? It's the perfect time for Jesus to come." Zag grins. "And maybe it's also the perfect time for him to save the people. Either way, Jesus is here."

"But if Jesus is the Messiah, don't the people just think he's going to save us from poverty and from Rome? They don't know why Jesus is really here." There's a knot in my stomach, and it's getting tighter by the minute.

"Yeah. But Abe, aren't you forgetting that God has a plan?"

He's right, but it doesn't make me feel better right now. I look down at the earth. I can see a city in the distance.

Zag asks me again, "Are you ready to go see Jesus?"

This is it. I've heard Dad, Grandpa, and our neighbors talk about Jesus so much for almost three years. I didn't think I was ever going to get to really see him. I remind myself to breathe, and I loudly answer, "Yes!"

Zag points to the still-turning earth. "We're almost there. Most people haven't heard about Jesus yet. But he changed some water into wine at a wedding, and people are starting to realize he's special. Word about him is spreading fast. He's in Jerusalem right now for the Jewish Passover."

"Is that where we're going . . . to Jerusalem?"

"Yes, but we won't be in the city. We'll be just outside it."

* * *

The earth stops, and my feet hit the ground. It's really dark out. I wonder where Jesus is and how I'm going to be able to see him. I'm so excited. I wonder if he'll be short or tall, skinny or fat. In my mind, I picture him being perfect in every way.

Zag points to a fire in the distance. "There," he says. "That's where he is. He's with a Pharisee named Nicodemus. I want you to hear what they're talking about."

We get closer, and I know immediately which one is Jesus. He's sitting on a rock, bent over with his elbows resting on his knees. He's talking to a man who's sitting on the ground, his back against a tree. Jesus's hands are clasped together in a soft grip. Then he holds out one hand to explain something.

His eyes are dark like his hair and beard. His gaze is gentle. I feel so drawn to him. There's so much emotion growing inside me, I almost want to cry. But yet I feel peaceful—kind of like I felt in the garden of Eden. I love him like . . . like I love Mom or Dad or Grandpa. But different too. I can hear his voice now, soft and kind.

Zag bumps my shoulder and whispers, "Listen."

I was planning to!

"I know you must come from God," Nicodemus says. "Nobody can do miracles like you are doing unless God is with him."

"You're right," Jesus replies. "I tell you, no one can see the kingdom of God if they're not born from above."

Nicodemus sits up straight and motions to his body. "But how can anybody be born when they're already grown? How is it possible for me to enter my mother's womb and be born again?"

"Listen. I'm telling you. Neither you nor anybody can enter the kingdom of God if you are not born of water and Spirit. Flesh is born from flesh, and Spirit is born from Spirit."

Nicodemus looks confused. So am I.

"Don't let this surprise you," Jesus continues. He drops his head for a moment like he's thinking. Then he looks up again, raises his hand in the air, and says, "The wind blows. You can feel it and even hear it. But you can't be sure where it comes from or where it goes. It's the same with being born of the Spirit."

Jesus keeps talking, but Nicodemus still seems confused.

"Remember the story of Moses lifting up the serpent in the desert? He told the people to look at it, and if they believed they would be healed."

Nicodemus nods his head. "Yes."

"Well, just like that snake, the Son of Man will be lifted up too. If anyone believes in him, they will have eternal life."

I'm not sure who the Son of Man is, but I think Jesus means himself.

Jesus holds out his hands toward Nicodemus. "Do you know how much God loves you, Nicodemus?" Jesus spreads his arms wide as he continues. "God loves the world so much that he's giving his Son—his *only Son*!—so nobody has to perish."

He drops his hands back into his lap and says, "Everyone can have eternal life. God didn't send his Son to condemn the world. He sent his Son to save the world. No one who believes will be condemned, but those who don't believe are already condemned."

I step back as Jesus stands up and moves closer to the fire. Nicodemus stands up too.

Jesus stares into the fire and says, "God is the light of the world. But people would rather choose darkness. People who do wicked and bad things hate the light. They hide in the dark. But good people who love truth and are kind welcome the light."

I start to feel bad for God, because he lost his perfect creation when Adam and Eve sinned. It must have been sad for God to watch evil and darkness spread across the earth. I wish people wouldn't choose darkness over light.

I'm glad God sent Jesus to save us. Then I realize that Jesus didn't say anything about *dying* to save the world. Maybe he won't have to die.

Zag takes my hand, and we float up. The fire gets smaller and smaller until it's gone. He doesn't say anything about what we just saw. Instead he says, "Jesus's teachings will be new to everybody. He'll need men who can learn from him, men who can become leaders of this new way. Jesus will call these men disciples. They'll follow him wherever he goes."

* * *

As the earth slows, I see Jesus standing at the edge of a big sea. He's watching two men in the water. The sand feels hot on my feet when we land. I step closer to the water and dig my toes down into the ground. They hit wet, cold sand. *Ugh!* I shake the wet sand off my feet and step back toward the hot, dry beach again.

Jesus is still watching the fishermen. We get fish from the market in Bethlehem, so I've never watched anyone fish before. They throw their net out over the water. It sinks down, and I watch them pull it back up with a rope. It closes like a bag—I guess so any fish they catch can't get away. But the net is empty. We watch them do this over and over, but still no fish.

I think Jesus might be tired of watching them not catch any fish, because he hollers, "Hey, guys! Come here! If you follow me, I'll make you fishers of men."

What?

But the two fishermen don't ask what he means—they don't even ask who he is. They just come out of the water and throw their net down on the sand.

Jesus smiles as he turns to walk down the shoreline. The two fishermen follow him.

I turn to Zag, amazed. "What made them just drop everything and follow Jesus?"

"Well," Zag says, "wouldn't you?"

I don't have to even think about that one. There is something about Jesus that just makes me feel like I'm bursting with love inside. He's kind and gentle and loving. Of course I would follow Jesus. "Okay, but who were they?" I ask.

"That was Simon and his brother, Andrew. Jesus will change Simon's name to Peter."

"Oh, like God changed Abraham and Israel's names?"

"Yep," Zag says. "Let's follow them."

I've never walked in sand like this before. Every step I take, my feet sink into the ground a little. Little waves of water roll up onto the sand, one after another. The water comes close but doesn't quite reach us. We're still following Jesus and the men. They're moving quickly. They're kicking up the sand behind them as they walk.

Jesus stops in front of a boat full of men working on nets.

"This is where two more brothers join Jesus," Zag says. "These are James and John."

I hear Jesus call them, but I can't hear what he's saying. And then these men get out of the boat and follow Jesus.

"Where are they going?" I ask.

"They're headed to Capernaum, where Simon and Andrew are from. Jesus will talk to the people there about the kingdom of God. He will also heal every person in Capernaum who is sick. After that, news about Jesus will spread like fire.

"Most of these people have lived in poverty for a long time. A lot of them are sick because they can't afford doctors. Hearing about Jesus gives them hope. People will walk for miles to be healed by Jesus. They'll also come because they'll hear he's the promised Savior."

"That's all good, right?"

"Well, it's not good for the leaders in Jerusalem. If Jesus gets too much attention, Rome will think he wants to be a king. That could change everything, and they have too much to lose. You'll see, Abe— the more people talk about Jesus, the more upset the leaders will get. They'll eventually plot to stop him."

Stop him? "But God has a plan . . . right?"

Zag smiles. "You've got it! You know, Jesus will have a lot of loyal followers. Thousands of people will walk miles just to see him. People will bring sick family and friends to Jesus to be healed. It seems impossible that Jesus can heal everybody, but he takes his time going through the crowds. He heals every single sick person."

Dad and Grandpa have always said that God is powerful and that he loves us, but nothing I've ever heard comes close to what I'm seeing and hearing now. I can't explain the emotion building up inside of me. I feel like God is pouring his love out on all the people through Jesus. And on me!

Zag interrupts my thoughts. "What do you say, should we go listen to Jesus teach?"

I grin. "Yes, I'd like that very much."

He takes my hand, and we're off again, watching the earth turn.

CHAPTER 4

TRUSTING THE PLAN

This time when the earth stops, I'm standing close to Jesus. His twelve disciples are there, and I recognize four of them from the shore. Most of them are sitting on big rocks, but two are standing. We're on the side of a mountain. We're high enough to see all the people who've come to see Jesus. There are so many! Where did they all come from?

I look back at Jesus. That love inside my chest is building up again.

Zag whispers, "You might want to sit. We'll be here a while."

I sit down on the ground, my eyes still focused on Jesus. Zag sits next to me. Jesus stands up and lifts his hand. The people are watching him too, and a hush moves through the crowd until everyone becomes quiet.

Jesus looks out at everyone with pure love and concern. He reaches both hands toward the people and says, "Blessed are those of you who are hurting or poor in spirit, for the kingdom of heaven is yours. And for any of you who are grieving, you will be comforted." He pauses.

"Blessed are you who are modest and humble, because you will inherit the earth."

I love how Jesus talks slowly and pauses a lot. It gives me time to think about what he says.

He turns to face the crowd on his left. "And all of you who are hungry and thirsty for justice, you will be satisfied. Those of you who are merciful, you yourselves will receive mercy." Another pause. "Those of you who are pure in heart, you will see God."

He turns to the people on the right and continues speaking. "If you choose to make peace, you will surely be called children of God. For those of you who are persecuted for doing and saying the right thing, yours is the kingdom of heaven."

Then he turns and faces the crowd straight ahead of him again. He spreads his arms toward his disciples and says, directly to them, "When people persecute you and say bad things about you because of me, be happy, because your reward is great in heaven."

I listen, soaking up every word he says. I look out at the crowd, and they're listening too.

"You've heard the saying, 'an eye for an eye and a tooth for a tooth'?" Jesus asks.

People nod, agreeing with him. I can even remember Grandpa saying that.

Jesus continues. "Do not argue with an evil, mean person. In fact, if someone slaps you on the right cheek, give him your other cheek to slap as well. And if anyone wants to sue you and take your coat, let him have your cloak too. If anyone makes you go one mile, offer to go a second mile."

Suddenly I shiver. I look over at the sun and realize the day is almost gone. I pull my knees to my chest and wrap my arms around them. Maybe I can hold in some of my heat.

Zag notices and whispers, "Do you want to move on?"

I shake my head no and go back to listening to Jesus.

"You've probably also heard that you should love your neighbor and hate your enemy, right?"

Again people nod in agreement.

Jesus says, "I'm telling you to love your enemies. Pray for the people who are mean to you. Then you'll be the children of your Father in heaven."

Jesus points up to the sky and says, "God allows the sun to rise both on the bad and on the good. He also sends rain on both the bad and the good. Don't just love the people who love you but love those who hate you."

I could listen to Jesus all day, but he stops talking. He walks down the mountain and into the crowd. His disciples follow him.

"So what do you think?" Zag asks.

"Everything Jesus says is good. It makes me feel good and makes me want to do good." I look at Zag and say, "It's easy to see that Jesus has a kind heart. He wants us to love each other and help each other."

"Yeah, I know." Zag peers over the heads of those around us to see Jesus in the crowd. "He is moving through the crowd, healing whoever is sick. What do you say we go see what happens when Jesus goes to his hometown of Nazareth?"

Oh, I'm sure the people in Nazareth will be proud of Jesus—who he is and what he's done. Excitedly, I say "Yes!"

* * *

I'm getting used to this traveling-through-time stuff. This time when we land, we're standing in front of a synagogue. This is where the community gathers to worship. I didn't expect to see Jesus at the synagogue. This is great. I'm sure Jesus will do the reading and teaching. We step inside the door, and it's so packed with people that there isn't a place to sit. I can see some of Jesus's disciples standing near him, up front. I'm glad so many have come to hear him teach.

Zag nudges me and points to a woman sitting in the back. He says, "That's Mary, Jesus's mother."

I've never seen such a quiet, gentle face. She's wearing a simple blue dress with a white-and-blue headcloth draped over her head. Her hands are clutched in her lap and her head is down, like she's praying.

I wonder what it's like for her to be the mother of Jesus. She must know Jesus is the Savior God promised to send. I whisper to Zag, "Does she know her Son is going to save our people?"

He smiles and says, "Yes, she does. But it's something she holds deep in her heart."

A commotion begins at the front of the room. I stand on my tiptoes and see Jesus opening a scroll and getting ready to read. I push my way through to the front and get as close as I can.

Jesus stands still and waits for everyone to stop talking. When it gets quiet, he unrolls the scroll a bit further and studies it. Then he reads from it.

"The Spirit of the Lord is upon me. He has anointed me to bring good news to the poor. He has sent me to proclaim liberty to those who are held captive and to give sight to those who are blind. He sends me to free those who are oppressed."

I can tell he's reading from Isaiah's writings. I can still picture Isaiah. He was so sad.

Jesus stops reading. We wait for him to read some more, but he slowly rolls up the scroll and sets it down. We all stare at Jesus and wait for him to say something. Finally, he looks up and says, "Today, just as you have heard me read it, this has all come to be. It has been fulfilled."

All I hear are gasps, like everyone is shocked he said that. People are whispering all around me, but I can't tell what anyone is saying.

Someone in the crowd says, "Where did this man get all this?"

The crowd gets louder, and another man shouts, "Hey! Isn't he Mary's son? He's the son of a carpenter!" The sarcastic tone of his voice is meant to be insulting.

Jesus doesn't say anything for a while. The crowd is getting louder and angrier. I feel bad for him. Then he holds up his hand and says, "You're right. I am Mary's son. And yes, it is true that I grew up here in Nazareth. But it's also true that no prophet is accepted in his hometown."

Well, now everybody's mad and they want Jesus to leave. In their rush to grab him, I get squashed. I yelp—loudly—when someone stomps on my foot, but no one can hear or see me. They're all yelling and pushing against each other trying to get at Jesus. It takes a while, but they finally get him out of the synagogue. The pushing and yelling don't stop.

Zag and I follow the angry crowd and watch as they push Jesus outside the city. I gasp when I realize they're pushing Jesus toward a cliff. *Oh no,* I think. *This must be it! They're going to kill Jesus. They're going to throw him over that cliff!*

They stop at the edge of the cliff. I can't see Jesus anymore.

I look to Zag for help, but he smiles and says, "Keep watching."

I do, but the wait is brutal. And then I see him—Jesus—calmly walking through the crowd and then away.

"Why were they so mean to Jesus?" I ask.

"They don't believe," Zag answers, "because they only see Jesus as Mary's son. In time they'll believe."

He takes my hand, and as we begin to move, he asks, "Have you ever heard how Jesus fed five thousand people at once? He fed them with only five loaves of bread and two fish!"

I watch the earth turn and remember a neighbor telling us that story.

"Yes," I reply, "but we didn't believe it. We thought someone made that one up."

Zag smiles at that. "Well, we're heading to Bethsaida. That's way out in the middle of nowhere."

The earth starts to slow down.

* * *

Thousands of people are listening to Jesus, and it's late in the day. I can feel the cool evening air as we land. I'm close enough to hear one of the disciples tell Jesus, "We're way out in the country, and it's late. Why don't you send the people away, so they can find something to eat?"

"They don't have to go anywhere to find something to eat," Jesus replies. "You can feed them right here."

The disciple's face shows his shock. Almost accusingly, he asks, "You want *us* to go buy food? It would take a whole year's wages to feed this many people!"

"Go see how many loaves of bread we have," Jesus answers.

The disciple stands there like he doesn't know how to respond. Even I can see they don't have enough bread to feed all these people. Why even look?

Jesus just repeats his instruction. "Go and see."

The disciple walks away to where all their personal things are. He comes back to Jesus, carrying a basket. He holds it out and says, "We have five loaves of bread and two fish."

Jesus takes the basket. He tells the disciples, "Have the people sit in groups of fifty and a hundred. That'll make it easier to pass out the food."

The disciples don't question Jesus this time. They start organizing the crowd just like he said. Before too long, more than half the crowd is organized, and the rest see what they're doing and move into groups themselves without being told.

Jesus raises the basket of food toward heaven and prays. Then he breaks the fish and bread and hands a portion to each disciple. They pass it on to the people and come back for more. They do this over and over until everybody is fed. Then Jesus tells them to go collect the leftovers. They do, and I can see there are more leftovers than there was food when they started.

I want to say I can't believe it, but I *saw* it happen!

Zag walks over and takes some bread and a big piece of fish from the leftovers. He hands it to me. "You must be starving," he says.

I hadn't thought about it until this moment, but suddenly I realize I *am* starving. I can't remember the last time I ate. But then, I don't know what day it is either.

"Mmm, thanks!" I say, and I start eating what might be the best bread and fish I've ever tasted.

It's getting dark now, and the people are settling in for the night.

Zag says, "I want you to hear what Jesus tells his disciples. They'll be alone in Caesarea Philippi. But first I want to show you something that happens tonight. We won't land. Instead, we'll just float above it. You'll see why."

My stomach is full and I'm feeling good, so all I say is, "Okay."

* * *

The earth hardly turns before it stops again. It's dark out, but the moon is bright. We're floating above a raging sea with waves that could pull us under. We're so close, the spray of the waves hits me, and I have to wipe the mist from my eyes.

There's a boat rolling back and forth between the waves. Zag points away from it and says, "Look!"

I follow his finger and see—is that Jesus walking on the water? I shake my head and look again. It is!

Just then, one of the disciples sees Jesus too. He screams, "Look, it's a ghost!" They all panic.

"Don't worry," Jesus calls out. "It's me, Jesus. Don't be afraid."

A disciple comes to the edge of the deck. I'm sure it's Simon. I recognize him from the shore. He stands there a minute, squinting his eyes to see. He hollers, "Jesus, is it really you? Call me to come to you. If it's really you, I'll walk over to you on the water."

Simon must be crazy! I wouldn't get out of that boat in these waves.

But Jesus says, "Come."

I almost can't watch. But then, I can't help but watch.

Simon climbs over the side of the boat and drops down to the water. He doesn't sink! He starts walking toward Jesus. He's almost there when a gust of wind hits him. He takes his eyes off Jesus to look at the waves, and he starts to sink. Fear overtakes him.

"Lord, save me!" he screams.

Jesus reaches out and grabs Simon's hand. The wind and waves are noisy, but somehow I can hear Jesus.

"Oh, Simon, you have so little faith," he says. "Why did you doubt?"

Hand in hand, Jesus and Simon walk together back to the boat. If Simon says anything to Jesus, I can't hear it. They climb into the boat, and instantly the sea calms down. And then the boat disappears.

"Zag!" I cry. "Where did the boat go?"

Zag shrugs his shoulders and says, "It's on the shore."

And I know this is hard to believe, but he's right. I don't know how it got there so fast, but the boat is on shore. I can see it.

The earth starts turning again.

"Let's go to Caesarea Philippi," Zag says. "I want you to hear something Jesus tells his disciples."

* * *

When the earth stops, I see the disciples sitting around a fire. Jesus is nearby, but he's alone, praying. He stands up and walks over to his men. They shuffle to make room by the fire and offer him a nice big rock to sit on. Jesus sits down, then leans forward to rest his arms on his knees. He folds his hands together and stares into the fire.

I can tell Jesus is thinking hard.

Finally, he looks up and asks, "Who do people say I am?"

One disciple answers, "John the Baptist."

Jesus smiles as he thinks about that.

"I've heard some say you're Elijah, come back from the dead," another disciple says.

Jesus nods his head.

"Umm, a lot of people are saying you're a prophet," someone else adds.

Jesus waits to hear more, but that's it. Very slowly, he looks around the circle, from one follower to the next. Softly he asks, "But who do *you* think I am?"

Simon stands up so fast he scares me, and I jump to the side. Boldly, he says, "You're the Messiah!"

That isn't news to me because Zag told me, but apparently it is to Jesus's disciples. They all seem a little surprised that Simon would say that.

Jesus motions for Simon to sit down. Looking right at him, he says, "Simon, you are blessed, because this was revealed to you by my Father in heaven." Everyone, including Simon, looks surprised at that.

Jesus pauses for a moment, then looks back at Simon. "Simon, you will be called Peter, which means *rock*. I will build my church on this rock and nothing will overcome it. Not even the gates of hell. Peter, I will give you the keys to the kingdom of heaven."

Everyone gasps a bit at that.

"Whatever you choose to bind on earth will be bound in heaven. Whatever you choose to loose on earth will be loosed in heaven."

It sounds to me like Jesus is making Peter the leader. But then Jesus surprises me.

"Do not reveal to anyone that I am the Messiah," he says.

Why?

"Zag!"—I have to ask it—"Why wouldn't he want everyone to know that?"

"If people know that, Abe, they'll try to make Jesus a king. I don't think that fits into God's plan right now."

"But—"

Zag shushes me and says, "Listen."

I listen, but Jesus isn't talking. He's bent over again, leaning on his knees and rubbing his hands together. It feels like he wants to say something, but he doesn't. The disciples just wait quietly.

Finally, Jesus says, "I will have to go through some pretty intense suffering. The elders, the chief priests, and even the scribes will come up against me."

The disciples start asking questions, all at the same time.

Jesus holds up his hand, motioning for them to calm down and listen. He takes a deep breath, and then he says it. "I will be killed."

Now the disciples are terrified. Some of them jump up, while others just sit there with their mouths open.

Jesus raises his hand again and waits for them to settle down. Then he finishes by saying, "But on the third day, I will rise up."

The men are all standing now, and so am I.

Isaiah said the same thing, but I was hoping God could somehow save Jesus.

Peter stomps back and forth like he's in a rage. Pointing his finger, he says, "God forbid it, Lord! We can't let this happen to you!"

I want to hug Peter. I agree with him.

But Jesus jumps up and spreads his hands downward. He closes his eyes tight. "Satan . . . get behind me!" he cries. "You will not make me fail."

I get so scared, I jump behind Zag.

Everybody stops right where they are. It's scary quiet.

Jesus turns to Peter with a pleading look on his face. "Peter, you are thinking like a human being thinks, not like God would," he says.

The tension in the air eases, and the disciples relax. They start comforting one another with hugs and pats on the back. They all sit back down, but I can't. I'm torn between not wanting Jesus to be killed and wanting God's plan to work.

Jesus is sitting on his rock again, leaning on his knees like before. I'm standing close enough to touch him, and I wonder if he knows I'm there. I wish I could hug him, but I can't. All I can do is look at him and love him.

Jesus spreads his arms out toward the disciples. "Look," he says. "If you want to be my followers, you have to deny yourselves. You have to take up your cross and follow me. If you want to save your life, you will lose it. But if you lose your life for my sake, I promise, you will find it."

He keeps talking, but I'm not listening anymore. I know he's right. I know for sure now that he has to die. My stomach feels sick. I have to stop hoping God will somehow save him. I have to stop wanting him to not die. I have to have faith in God's plan. But it's just so hard. I feel so numb and tired.

I realize Zag is holding my hand, and we're floating up away from them. I watch the earth turn and try to not think about anything. From far away, I hear Zag talking.

"I want you to see something your dad will talk about when you get home," he says.

I still feel sick, but the thought of seeing Dad and Grandpa perks me up. "You mean I can see Dad and Grandpa in the future? No, wait." I am so confused. "Is it the future or the past?"

Zag laughs at me. "They're going to Bethany. Two sisters who live there sent word for Jesus to come and heal their sick brother, Lazarus. Most of the people will be from Jerusalem, because Bethany is only two miles from there. I'm sure we'll see a few leaders in the crowd too."

I think out loud. "I wish the leaders would just stay home. I want them to leave Jesus alone. He isn't doing anything to hurt anyone. He's teaching people to be kind and healing people who are sick."

Zag just smiles as he says, "I know what you mean."

* * *

There are crowds of people below us. I look for Dad and Grandpa.

"We're not going to land yet," Zag says. "Let's just float awhile. You okay with that?"

That's fine with me. I shrug and continue scanning the crowd for my family. Zag sees them first and points them out.

There they are, and Uncle Jacob is with them. They're all tall. They won't have any trouble seeing over the crowd. I suddenly realize I've missed them, but I'm glad I didn't find them that night. I would never have experienced this great adventure I'm on.

Now I look for Jesus.

Zag knows what I'm thinking again, because he says, "Jesus isn't here yet. In fact, Lazarus has been dead for four days."

"What? Wouldn't Jesus know that? Maybe he's not coming."

"You do remember there isn't anything God can't do, right?" Zag raises an eyebrow and gives me a funny grin like he's waiting for me to say he's right.

I do, but if that's true, I wonder, *why can't God save Jesus from dying?* I'm starting to feel sad again and force myself to stop thinking about it.

Suddenly, I see Dad pointing at something. I look over just in time to see a woman running toward the house.

"Jesus is here," she calls out. She stops and grabs the arm of a woman who could almost be her twin. "He's asking for you." They both run off, and the crowd follows them.

"That's Mary and Martha," Zag explains.

We're still floating above the crowd, and we watch as the sisters find Jesus. They fall down in front of him, and both are crying.

"Oh, Lord," they cry, "if you would have been here, our brother would not have died."

Jesus takes their hands and cries with them. "Where have you laid him?" he asks.

The sisters lead Jesus to a tomb. The crowd follows.

Zag and I are still floating. Dad, Grandpa, and Uncle Jacob are at the front of the crowd. I'm glad they're close enough to hear whatever Jesus is going to say. Zag and I touch down right next to Jesus, and I can't believe what I hear him say.

"Take away the stone."

One of the sisters puts her hand over her mouth to cover her gasp. "But Jesus," she says, "It will smell. He's been dead for four days."

Jesus looks at her, and I can tell he loves her. He says, "Didn't I tell you to believe? If you believe, I promise, you will see God's glory!"

She hesitates, then motions for some men to push the big stone away. The sisters begin to cry again, but Jesus looks up to heaven and starts to speak.

"Father, I thank you for hearing me. I know you hear me, but I want those here to know that too. I want them to believe that you sent me."

Then Jesus stretches his hands toward the tomb and hollers, "Lazarus, come out!"

The crowd is absolutely still. We're all holding our breath and staring at that tomb. We wait in silence, and then—there he is. We all see him.

Lazarus is standing at the entrance of the tomb. I take a deep breath at the sight of him. I can't take my eyes off him. Every person in the crowd is overwhelmed at what they're seeing. Lazarus doesn't move. He can only stand there, because his whole body is wrapped tight in white cloth.

"Pull those cloths off of him," Jesus says, "and let him go."

Jesus's face is full of love and kindness. I don't know when I came to love him so much, but every time I see him, I just love him more. The crowd isn't quiet anymore. In fact, a lot of them are down on their knees, praising God. Even Dad, Grandpa, and Uncle Jacob are.

If these people didn't believe in Jesus before, they do now.

"Nobody can say Jesus isn't the Messiah after seeing that, Zag!" I'm so excited, I just want to shout it out.

"You're right, but that just makes things worse for Jesus." Zag shakes his head and points to the crowd. "All these people will go back to Jerusalem, and this is all they'll talk about. There won't be a person in Jerusalem who won't be talking about Jesus."

"But . . . how is that bad?"

"This can only help the high priest Caiaphas to convince the leaders."

"Convince them of what?"

"If they do nothing to stop Jesus," Zag explains, "Rome will. They'll destroy the temple and the nation."

"But . . . no, Zag! Jesus came to save them, not to destroy them. I heard him say so myself."

"Yeah, but fear makes people do things they wouldn't normally do. Believe me, the Jewish leaders are afraid of Jesus. Just a small suggestion from Caiaphas will get them planning and plotting."

I shiver. "What will he suggest?"

"That it's better for one man to die for the people than to have the whole nation destroyed."

"What?! They've got it all wrong!" I scream. "Jesus is supposed to die to save us from sin! If Caiaphas gets his way, no one will know that."

"Abe, you have to have faith in God's plan."

"I know, but it's really hard to do that sometimes."

Zag reaches for my hand, and the crowd disappears below us. The earth starts to turn again, and Zag tilts his head and looks my way. "I hate to say this," he says, "but our adventure is over."

I wasn't expecting that, and my heart drops a little. Of course, I know this can't go on forever, but neither do I want it to end. Suddenly,

I wonder how long I've been gone. I have no idea. I wonder if Adam ever figured out I didn't go home.

Oh, this whole adventure will be hard to explain. What do I say about where I've been?

But once again, Zag reads my mind. "We'll be getting back at the perfect time. Your brother will just be coming in from the fields with the sheep. Your dad and grandpa will just be coming home from their journey. You'll meet them both where the path breaks off for the main road.

"Your dad and grandpa will think you've been with your brother, your brother will think you've been home with your mom, and your mom will think you've been in the field with your brother. Nobody knew you were missing, so nobody had to worry."

That's just amazing! I think. But then I feel guilty, like I've done something wrong.

"Shouldn't I still tell them what happened and where I've been?" I worry.

"Of course you should," Zag says.

There's so much to tell, I don't know what to tell them first. And if I start by telling them how I left Adam to go find Dad and Grandpa, Dad will be mad! I want to tell them, but I'm afraid to.

Zag laughs. "Believe me, Abe. Everything will work out fine at home."

"Really?"

He laughs again. "Yeah, because nobody will believe you."

Well, that just makes me sad. "Even Grandpa won't believe me?" I ask.

Zag squeezes my hand. "Not at first, but eventually they all will." He gives me a quick hug and says, "Time to go home."

CHAPTER 5

THE ADVENTURE IS OVER

The sun is getting low in the west, but there are still a couple hours of daylight left. Our feet touch the ground, and Zag says, "Right where we started from. Look," he points behind us. "There's that path that takes you to the main road." I'm shocked and say, "That's exactly where I said goodbye to Dad and Grandpa!"

I remember how mad I was at myself that night when I felt lost. Now, I'm glad I did get lost.

Zag points in the opposite direction. "You'll want to walk in that direction. Your brother will be coming over that hill any minute now. As soon as you join him, you'll see your dad and grandpa coming up that path." He snaps his fingers and adds, "Oh, and one more thing— Jesus is heading to Jerusalem for the last time. If you want to see him again, you'll have to convince your dad to take you. And soon!"

He puts his arm around my shoulders and says, "This was a fun adventure, Abe. I'm glad we got to do it, but now I have to go."

I know Zag has to leave before anybody shows up, but I wish he could stay. I hug him as tight as I can. "Thank you, Zag. Thank you so much. You showed me so many things—everything has changed for me. I don't want to say goodbye." Even saying the word makes me sad.

Zag laughs as he hugs me back.

I push away. "What's so funny?"

"This isn't goodbye, Abe. I promise I will always be wherever you are, watching out for you." He gives me a thumbs-up, and in that moment, he's gone.

I turn and walk in the direction my brother Adam will be coming from. I can't wait to tell my family all the stories . . . but I'm afraid to, too. I disobeyed Dad, *and* I lied to Adam. But so much has happened! I hope I can remember it all. I hope Dad will take me to see Jesus. If we wait too long to go see him, it might be too late.

A ewe and two little lambs bound over the top of the hill. Right behind them comes Adam, surrounded by the rest of our sheep. I don't want to make them scatter, so I carefully push my way through and over to Adam.

"Good to see you, Abe," he says, giving me a shoulder-to-shoulder hit that almost knocks me into the sheep. "I guess you found your way home the other night."

Oh, man! What do I say?

Before I can think of an answer, Adam points down the hill. "Hey, look! There's Dad and Grandpa!"

The sheep are already making the turn to head home. We let them go and walk over to meet Dad and Grandpa coming up the path from the main road.

I am so glad to see them, Dad especially. I throw my arms around him and hug him for a long time. Dad is really tall, so my face is pushed against his chest. With a muffled voice I say, "I missed you! I'm so glad you're home." Dad's long arms return the hug.

He lets go of me when Adam reaches out to shake Dad's hand.

"How was the trip?" Adam asks. "Did you get to see Jesus?"

Dad nods, and Adam turns to Grandpa. "So do you think Jesus is the one you saw thirty years ago?"

I don't want to ask any of those questions. It doesn't feel right when I know the answers.

I can't even guess at how many days I've been gone. I should have asked Zag. I'm so hungry! And tired. I could sleep right here standing on my feet.

Dad's voice startles me, and I realize I've not been paying attention. "Boys," he says, pointing to the sheep. "Are we going to let the animals beat us home?" They've gotten way ahead of us. We all start walking faster than I'd like, just to catch up with the sheep.

"It was an unbelievable trip," Dad says. "Uncle Jacob joined us, and yes, we did see Jesus. We found him at Bethany. What he did there was amazing, but we'll talk about that later. When Jesus left Bethany, we followed him. He went across the Jordan River and over into Perea. We listened to him teach. He is an amazing teacher."

Dad leans forward to see around me and says, "Next question is yours, Grandpa."

Grandpa shakes his head a little and takes a deep breath. Exhaling, he says, "Yes, Adam, Jesus is that baby I saw thirty-some years ago. And yes, there is no doubt in my mind he is the promised Messiah."

Adam's eyes are wide. "Wow!" He's a little breathless. "So you don't regret making that trip?"

"No!" "Not at all!" Grandpa and Dad answer at the same time.

Dad looks at me and says, "In fact, Abe, I'm sorry we didn't let you come with us, because we didn't run into anything or anyone who would give us reason to fear for our safety."

I don't care that he didn't let me go with him. All I can think about is what Zag said. Jesus is coming back to Jerusalem one last time. I want to see him again before it's too late. I have to ask. I jump in front of Dad and start walking backward. "Dad, can I go see him? I really want to see him. We can just go to Jerusalem and that's it. I won't ask you to take me anywhere else. Please?"

Dad and Grandpa look at each other, smiling. Dad's deep voice is husky as he says, "Yes."

"Really?" In my excitement, I grab him and almost knock him over. "Oh, thank you, Dad! Thank you!"

Dad laughs and catches his balance. I let go and move to his side.

"Well, we'll have to figure out a few things first, before we leave."

"Like what?"

"To begin with, your mother can't travel. And then there's Passover coming up."

I can't help but ask the obvious, "Dad, why can't we try to take Mom with us? Jesus could heal her."

"I've considered that, Abe." Dad gets a sad look on his face. "But your mom isn't strong enough to make that trip."

Adam breaks the awkward silence. "Our neighbors at the creek invited us to join them for Passover. I'll take Mom there for Passover, and I can take care of the sheep." He shrugs his shoulders and gives Dad a look of *what else?*

I look back at Dad and wait for him to answer.

"Adam," he says, "I'm really proud that I can count on you to help out. Are you sure you don't want to go see Jesus?"

"No." Adam shrugs. "That's okay. I'll see him another time."

Now I feel guilty, because I don't think there's going to be another time.

"Well, then that takes care of all my concerns." Dad looks at me. "I guess you, Grandpa, and I are going to Jerusalem."

But this is Adam's last chance to see Jesus too. Maybe I should let him go, since I did get to see Jesus with Zag.

"Oh. Umm, but Adam, are you sure you don't want to go? What if you don't get another chance to see Jesus?"

They all look at me with puzzled expressions on their faces.

"What are you talking about? Of course there'll be another chance to see Jesus." Dad ruffles the hair on my head. "I'm sure Jesus will be in Jerusalem for the Passover. We'll stay with your uncle Jacob. This will be your first long visit to Jerusalem, Abe. We can take our time to see things that we've never had time for before."

Grandpa interrupts, his eyes shining. "And I can take you on a personal tour of Jerusalem. There's a lot to do, and you know I'll have a story for everything we see."

Adam laughs and hits me on the shoulder. "There you go, Abe. I've done that tour before. Now it's your turn." He takes off running to open the sheep pen. They got home ahead of us and are wandering all around the house and yard.

There's a wagon with an ox hooked up to it by the shed. That's our neighbor from the creek who was staying with Mom. But there's another wagon with a mule hooked up to it in front of the house. That's our neighbor two hills over.

"Looks like our neighbors are here, hoping to hear about our trip," Grandpa says.

"I hope that's all it is." Dad's face looks worried. "Dad, why don't you help the boys with the sheep. I'm going to go in to make sure everything is okay."

Grandpa gives Dad a wave and walks toward the sheep. I do most of the running to round up the sheep, while Grandpa and Adam push them toward the pen. We all work well together and get most of the sheep in the pen.

Grandpa points to some strays running off. I chase after them and, in no time, have them running toward Grandpa and Adam. They're the last ones to go into the pen. Adam closes the gate and makes his nightly count. None are missing.

We all head to the shed. Inside, Adam and I climb the ladder up through a small opening and into the haymow. Without thinking, I grab a rake to push hay out for the sheep. Hay has never been scary to me before, but now, all I can think about is trying to catch my breath in that mud pit.

I don't hear Adam when he says, "That's enough."

I jump when he grabs the rake from my hand.

"That's enough, Abe! Let's get some water for the sheep."

I come to my senses and answer, "Yeah."

The well is between the house and the shed, and there are six buckets on the ground. It makes me think about the well in Egypt. I know I should tell Dad what I did. I know he'll be mad that I tried to follow him. But I don't want to tell him tonight with our neighbors here. I'll tell him tomorrow.

Grandpa lowers the well-bucket down into the well then turns the crank to pull it back up, full of water. He pours the water into one of the six buckets on the ground. He lowers the well-bucket back into the well again. After Grandpa fills a second bucket, Adam carries them to the watering trough without spilling a drop. I get the next two. I'm usually really good at getting the water to the trough without spilling it, but tonight is different. I'm too tired to be doing this. Adam laughs at me for spilling so much. Grandpa just raises his eyebrows at me. I lose track of how many trips we make, but finally the trough is full.

Grandpa holds the well-bucket up and says, "Abe, you first."

I bend over, and he slowly pours water over my head. The water is cold, but I rub it onto my hair, my neck, and my face. I stand up to wash my arms and hands. I can't wait to get in the house and warm up.

Grandpa and Adam finish washing up too, then Adam fills all six buckets one last time. They each take two buckets to carry back to the house. I look down at the two buckets left for me. Considering all the water I wasted a few minutes ago, I should probably make two trips, but I'm freezing. I pick up both buckets and shuffle toward the house.

I'm halfway to the house when Grandpa asks, "You okay, Abe?"

"Yeah," I grunt.

The door shuts behind Grandpa and Adam. When I finally get to the house, I set my now half-filled buckets down next to the four full ones. I stare at them and my wet legs. I think about the girl who spilled water on me in Egypt.

"Thank you, God, for saving the Hebrews," I mumble quietly.

Cold, wet, tired, and hungry, I open the door. *Home!* Warm air greets me. The brightly lit lamps make me realize how dark it is outside. Mom's in her favorite chair with a blanket over her lap. I can't resist her smile and walk over to her for a big hug. I whisper in her ear so no one can hear me, "I missed you, Mom."

She doesn't know I was supposed to be home the last couple days. I try not to feel guilty.

A neighbor lady arranges dishes on the table. Another sets out a big pot of stew. Steam rolls up out of the pot—it smells delicious. A fire crackles in the fireplace, making the house feel warm and cozy. It feels good to soak in that heat.

Someone says, "It's time to eat." I head for my normal spot, but Dad taps my shoulder.

"Abe, you'll have to take your food and sit by the fire. There isn't room for all of us to sit at the table."

I count eight sitting at the table, including my brother. I'm older than the neighbor kids who are here, but I'm still not old enough to get a seat at the full table.

Oh well. I won't let it bother me because *I'm* going to Jerusalem to see Jesus! I get my bowl of stew and hurry to claim Mom's big chair.

The neighbor kids will have to find places to sit on the floor around the fireplace.

Dad and Grandpa tell their stories between mouthfuls of food. Nobody wants to miss a word. We all live in the hills and don't get a lot of news. When someone comes home from visiting a different place, everyone wants to hear about what they've seen. We get together to hear it at the same time.

We've been hearing about Jesus for three years now, and a lot of what we've heard is almost too hard to believe. Or it was for me, before I met Zag. I'm listening closely.

"I'm convinced now," Grandpa says, "that Jesus is that baby I saw thirty years ago."

"But," one of the neighbors asks, "do you think he's the promised Messiah?"

"Yes, without a doubt."

The women, including Mom, clasp their hands in victory and murmur praise to God. I can see a look of hope and joy shine on their faces. It's beautiful.

The neighbor men start talking at once.

"We want to hear what Jesus did and what he said."

"Did he do any miracles?"

"Let me talk!" Grandpa says. "The first time we saw Jesus was at Bethany. He went to see two sisters named Mary and Martha. We heard their brother Lazarus was dying and that they'd asked Jesus to come. People said they were Jesus's good friends, so we figured he might show up."

I lean over and set my empty bowl on the floor. I'm still cold, so I pull Mom's blanket around me. I lean my head against the chair and listen to Grandpa.

"By the time we got there, Lazarus was dead. He'd already been in the tomb for four days. There were a lot of people there, but no Jesus. We were just about to leave when we saw one of the sisters—Martha, I believe—running to the house. She told Mary that Jesus had come."

I close my eyes and can see it happening. I even see the tears falling on Jesus's cheeks. I feel like I'm floating again, but it's too dark to see the earth turning.

Next thing I know, Dad's shaking my shoulder. I guess I fell asleep. I missed all their stories. I can't believe I slept through the noise of the neighbors leaving. I really am tired! I blink and look up at Dad.

"Time to go to bed, Abe," he says kindly. "We'll be heading out for Jerusalem in the morning."

I'm so warm under Mom's blanket, I don't want to move. Dad shakes me again, so I get up. I climb the ladder to the sleeping loft. It's warm up here. It catches all the heat from the fireplace, and tonight I'm glad. I change into my nightclothes and crawl into bed.

It feels so good . . . I'm so tired . . .

CHAPTER 6

RIDING A COLT

"Hey! Abe, wake up." Adam pokes me. It's not a nice way to wake up. "Did you forget you're going to Jerusalem today?"

Oh! I sit up, feeling like I had just fallen asleep.

Adam laughs. "Man, you fell asleep in that chair last night, and now I have to wake you up. I'm beginning to think you haven't slept for a couple days."

He doesn't know how right he is.

"You'd better hurry. Dad and Grandpa are waiting for you."

That wakes me up and gets my heart racing. I pull on my clothes and crawl down the ladder as fast as I can. Three bags are waiting by the door. They must be our clothes for the next few days. I wonder how long we're going to stay, but I don't ask because I don't want to ruin anything.

Mom is back in her chair under her blanket. I kiss her forehead and tell her good morning. Then I race to the table and sit down. A bowl of porridge is waiting for me, and it's not hot anymore. That's okay, because I can eat it faster.

I just finish scooping up the last bite when Grandpa and Dad open the door.

"Hmm, I thought maybe you were going to stay home and sleep," Dad says jokingly.

I wipe my mouth and push back from the table. "No. I'm ready."

Dad walks over to Mom. "We'll stay in Jerusalem to celebrate the Feast of Unleavened Bread. Then we'll be home. I love you."

Mom reaches up to put her hand on Dad's face. "I love you too. And be careful."

Right away, I realize we'll be there for more than a week. The Feast of Unleavened Bread is celebrated for eight days. Wow! That's more than I hoped for.

"Adam won't be taking the sheep to the pasture while we're gone," Dad says. "He'll be here if you need anything." He bends over and gives Mom a kiss and squeezes her hand.

Then he turns to me. "Ready, son?" He points to the bags by the door. "The small one is yours. Bring it here."

I do, and he turns me around and ties it on my back. Then he and Grandpa throw the other two bags over their shoulders, and out the door we go.

We're walking along the same dirt path I kicked rocks down just a couple days ago. We get to the turn where we said goodbye, but this time, I get to turn with them and walk down the hill. I let myself drop back a couple steps so Dad and Grandpa can't see me. Then I look up, smiling, and give Zag a thumbs-up. I know he can see me.

And in that moment, the guilt hits me because I haven't told Dad what I did. I know if I tell him, he'll probably send me home. But even if he doesn't send me home, I'm still afraid to tell him. I disobeyed him. I decide to wait, but it's all I can think about. Every step I take is one step closer to telling him.

We come to the main road. We turn right to go to Jerusalem. Just making that turn makes it feel real. We're going to see Jesus!

"Dad, do you think we'll get to see Jesus today?"

"I'm hoping we can. We'll wait and see what your uncle says. He'll know where to find Jesus if he's there."

I should be more excited, but all I feel is guilt. We keep walking, and no one is talking. I know waiting to tell Dad is wrong, but . . . what if he sends me home?

No, I can't wait any longer. I have to tell him the truth. I take a deep breath. "Dad, I have something to tell you."

Dad doesn't miss a step. "What is it, Abe?"

"Remember when you and Grandpa left to go see Jesus?"

"Yes."

"And remember I wanted to go with you, but you had Adam and me go to the field with the sheep?"

"Yes, Abe. What are you trying to say here?"

I clear my throat and take a deep breath. "Well, we got the sheep to the pasture, and I gathered wood for a fire." I kick a rock down the path in front of me. "And . . . and then I left."

"What do you mean, you left? You went home?"

"No. Adam thought I was going home, but I didn't. I tried to catch up to you and Grandpa. But I got lost."

Dad turns and looks straight at me. I look down at my feet so I don't have to see his angry face.

"Abe, if I had known this earlier—"

"I know, Dad! I know I should have said something before, but I was afraid to. I really did want to tell you everything that happened, but Zag said you wouldn't believe me."

Dad stops dead in his tracks and puts his hands on his hips. "Who is Zag?"

Just the thought of being able to tell him about my adventure gets me excited again. I forget about Dad being mad.

"He's my angel. The night I got lost, he found me and took me back to the beginning. The earth turned, and I saw Adam and Eve and all kinds of things."

"Whoa," Dad says. "You must have had one good dream."

"No, Dad. It was real. I even saw you and Grandpa in the crowd with Jesus. Really, I did."

Grandpa lets out a little chuckle, and Dad gives him a *this-isn't-funny* look.

"Okay, Abe. Slow down. We'd been talking about Grandpa seeing those angels, and then we left to go find Jesus. It's all stuff that's been in your head. When you're out in the field sleeping under the stars, you fall asleep faster than you realize. All this stuff comes into your dreams."

"But, Dad, it was *real*."

"Abe, stop." Dad stops talking and looks like he's deep in thought.

I'm afraid to say anything more.

Grandpa finally breaks the silence. "Abe, what you did was wrong."

Dad clears his throat. "Grandpa is right. You have to be punished."

I hold my breath and beg with my eyes not to go home. I know what I did was wrong. I brace myself for what I'm going to hear.

And then Dad says, "Just not now."

I exhale like I just got a second chance at life. I don't know what to say, so I stay quiet. Dad starts walking again, and we go without talking for a long time.

Finally, Grandpa says, "We're almost there."

I've been expecting to see Jerusalem from every hill we climbed. But now I see it. Wow! I feel like I'm seeing it for the first time. It's huge! There is a wall wrapped around two very high hills, and in the valley between them is Jerusalem.

Tents dot the hillside outside the walls. Dad chuckles as he points to them. "Those are people who've come for the Feast of Unleavened Bread and Passover. They don't have an Uncle Jacob to stay with."

The road is getting steep, and soon we're walking right up next to the wall. I let my hand rub against it as we walk. I think about when I ran through the Red Sea with my hand against the wall of water. This wall is made of thick, golden-brown stones that have been repaired in a lot of places.

Grandpa sees me touching the wall. "That's why they call this the Golden City, because of the color of those stones."

I realize Grandpa knows a lot.

We're all breathing hard climbing this hill. We finally reach a gate in the wall at the top of the hill.

Some officials stop us at the gate. Dad pulls me to the side while Grandpa talks to them. Then he argues with them. I start to worry, what if they don't let us in? I don't want to go home now!

"What's happening?" I ask Dad.

"This is a customs station. We have to pay tax on anything we take in or out of the city."

"All we have are our clothes," I protest. "Will they make us go home?"

"I think that's what Grandpa is arguing about," Dad replies.

I can't stand to watch them. The argument seems to go on forever. I step closer and try to hear what they're saying, but Dad pulls me back.

Finally, Grandpa walks back over to us. "Let's go before they decide to kick us out," he says, and we start moving quickly.

I'm half walking and half running to keep up with Dad and Grandpa. I look back to see if they're coming after us and nearly trip. The street is taking us down the hill into the valley. Finally we turn a corner, and I relax because I can't see them anymore.

Dad and Grandpa must feel better too, because we all slow down.

"I refuse to pay tax on clothes we're going to wear while we're here," Grandpa grumbles. "They even told me we have to spend ten percent of our income while we're here. That's not a Roman law. That's our own leaders making rules to get more money out of us. And that ten percent is over and above what we'll pay for our tithe at the temple." Grandpa is really upset.

I pat him on his back. "It's okay, Grandpa. You got us through the gate."

He looks at me and realizes how upset he is. He takes a deep breath, exhales, and smiles at me. "You're right, Abe," he says. "We're in."

We turn onto another street. It's really narrow, and the two-story houses are small. They're all connected with walls or steps. Kids are everywhere, running and having fun. Dad says this is where the poor people live.

We make another turn. The houses get a little bigger, but they're all still connected. Grandpa points to a house down the street. "There's Uncle Jacob's house," he says. "And look. There he is, sitting on the roof, watching for us." Grandpa gives him a big wave with both arms.

Uncle Jacob runs down some steps and yells into the house, "They're here!" Then he hurries up the street to greet us.

Uncle Jacob and Grandpa hug first and keep patting each other on their backs.

Dad hugs my uncle next. "It's good to see you again." Then he turns to me and says, "This is Abe. He's grown quite a bit since you last saw him."

Uncle Jacob holds his hand out to shake my hand. "My, what a young man you've become."

I can't wait any longer. I shake his hand and, without a hello, ask, "Is Jesus in Jerusalem?"

My uncle is still holding my hand. He looks up at Dad and grins.

Dad shrugs his shoulders. "He wants to see Jesus."

My uncle puts his arm around my shoulders. "Well, Abe, I hear he's in Bethany. That's just two miles away. He could show up any minute."

My mouth opens with a deep gasp. At the moment nothing else matters. Impatiently I ask, "Can we go see him? Can we, Uncle Jacob? Can we, Dad?"

I'm not sure why they all laugh at that. Uncle Jacob puts his hand on my back to lead us into his house. "I suppose we could go to the Mount of Olives and wait for Jesus to come by. Aunt Sarah's already packed us a lunch, so we can wait all day if you want to."

"You're the best!" I say as I hug Uncle Jacob as hard as I can. I don't think he hears me, because I almost knock him over. I have to remember I'm probably too old and too tall to be doing that.

He catches his balance and motions for me to go into the house. A lady with a baby and a boy I'm guessing is two years old greets us. Uncle Jacob introduces us. "This is Aunt Sarah. She's holding your cousin Ruth."

Grandpa taps Ruth's chin. "Abe, this is the first girl in the family," he says proudly.

Uncle Jacob smiles at Grandpa, then turns to introduce me to the little boy. "And this is your cousin Jeremiah."

Jeremiah looks at me shyly, but he runs to Grandpa and gives him a big hug. Grandpa picks him up and says, "Jeremiah, this is your cousin Abe. He came here to see Jesus."

Just hearing *Jesus* makes me want to leave right away.

Dad can tell, because he gives me a stern look. "Abe, just give us a minute to say hello."

I walk over to the fireplace and compare their house to ours. It seems the same but a little bigger. One big room to cook, eat, and relax by a fire. In the back are two rooms for sleeping. That's the same as ours. But instead of a ladder, they have steps. And instead of a loft, they have a whole second floor.

Grandpa puts Jeremiah down. He almost runs me over on his way to show Grandpa his wood blocks on the floor.

I give up waiting and sit down to watch him play. I feel a little jealous because I get called by a short name and he doesn't.

Finally Dad turns to me and asks, "Ready to go find Jesus?"

I jump up. "Yes! I can't wait."

"Let's get rid of this first." He unties the bag from my back. I'd almost forgotten I was carrying it.

Grandpa and I follow Uncle Jacob and Dad up the street. As we make a turn, I think I see the temple.

Grandpa points to it. "The temple is up there, but what you're seeing right now is the Temple Mount."

We're only a few blocks away from the Temple Mount when Uncle Jacob turns right. We walk through a gate and out to a wide road leading us down the hill into a valley.

"This is called the Kidron Valley." Uncle Jacob points to the top of the hill on the other side of the valley. "Up there is the Mount of Olives, and that's where we're headed."

I'm out of breath when we come to another road at the top of the hill.

Uncle Jacob goes left. "This wall runs all along the east side of Jerusalem," he explains. We walk a little farther and find a road going off to the right. "That road will take you to Bethany. That's where Jesus will be coming from."

I look down the road and see no sign of anybody coming.

"The Mount of Olives is just up here a little farther." Uncle Jacob says.

"What if Jesus is already here?" I ask.

"If he were here, I would know." He winks at me. "I have this friend, Zedekiah, who knows everything."

We follow Uncle Jacob into a grove of olive trees. He says, "If we stay on that road, it'll take us right past a cutoff that takes you back down the hill to the Golden Gate." He nudges me. "That's the gate Jesus uses. He'll pass right by us."

There are a lot of people in the olive grove. Uncle Jacob says, "I'm sure they're waiting for Jesus too. Let's find a place to sit in the shade. We'll still have a good view of the road to Bethany."

Grandpa finds a big rock to sit on.

I don't take my eyes off that road until Dad nudges me a few minutes later.

"Take a look at the crowd, Abe. There are chief priests, Sadducees, and Pharisees here."

"Who?" I ask. I mean, I think they're the ones who don't like Jesus, but I still don't know why. "Who are they?"

Uncle Jacob laughs, "Good luck explaining that one, brother!"

"Well, how can I answer that the shortest way?" Dad rubs his chin. "You know what a chief priest is. The Pharisees believe there is life after death. They believe in angels and that we should pay attention to old traditions and what the prophets said."

I must agree with the Pharisees, because I know there are angels.

"And the Sadducees"—he throws his hands up—"they don't believe in any of that. They only follow the Torah." Dad pauses. "You know the Torah is the law of God as revealed to Moses. Right, Abe?"

Of course I know that! I just nod my head. I'm still wondering why the Sadducees don't believe there are angels.

Uncle Jacob laughs again. "Well said!"

"Look!" Dad points to some people in the crowd. "You can tell them apart. The chief priests and Sadducees are dressed real fancy. They look rich. The Pharisees are dressed more like normal people."

Looking back and forth at them in the crowd confuses me. None of them look like they're mean. I don't understand why they can't just leave Jesus alone.

We wait about an hour, then eat our lunch. We wait a few more hours, and my legs start to hurt. It was a long walk to Jerusalem, and standing here for so long isn't easy. But I can't sit. I want to be the first to see Jesus.

I recognize two of Jesus's disciples coming up the road. They're leading a colt and make the turn to go to Bethany. Without thinking, I say, "Hey, aren't those two of Jesus's disciples with that colt?" *Oh! I shouldn't have said that!*

"Oh, you're right," Uncle Jacob says. "I wonder where they're going with that colt, and why?"

"The prophet Zechariah said our Savior will come riding on a colt," Grandpa says quietly. "I expect that colt is for Jesus."

That gets me excited, but Dad gives me a puzzled look. He shakes his head. "Okay, I have to ask. How did you know those two men were Jesus's disciples?"

I stare at him with my mouth open. Nothing comes out.

Grandpa laughs. "Maybe he saw them in his dream."

Dad smiles at Grandpa but looks back at me and waits for an answer.

Just then, someone in the crowd hollers, "There he is!"

"That's him," Uncle Jacob agrees. "He's riding on that colt those two disciples came by with."

The whole crowd rushes over to see Jesus. There are so many people, I can't even see the road anymore. I step up on a rock to see Jesus. He's wearing the same white garment with a brown sash tied around his waist. He's wearing a robe on top.

All those times I saw Jesus, I never noticed his soft, red robe. It's plain-looking, but somehow it makes him look like a king. He still has that kind, gentle face that makes me love him.

The disciples try to clear a path for Jesus so the colt can keep moving. The crowd backs off a little. It looks like they're laying something on the path in front of him. Then I realize they're laying their robes on the road. I shake Dad's shoulder.

"Dad, look! The people are throwing their robes on the ground in front of Jesus."

Then some people start pulling branches off the trees, and they lay them in the road too. Everyone is shouting.

"Blessed is the king. He comes in the name of the Lord!"

"Hosanna in the highest heavens!"

"Blessed be the king!"

"Blessed is the coming kingdom of our ancestor David!"

These people love Jesus, and they're doing what they can to honor him. Suddenly, I'm overcome by a wave of love for Jesus. Warm tears run down my cheeks. Dad puts his hand on my shoulder. I don't take my eyes off Jesus. "I see him, Dad. I really see him."

"I know how you feel, son. I truly believe he is the Savior, sent from God."

Jesus is on the main road now. He's heading toward the cutoff that will take him to the Golden Gate. People are still throwing down their robes and branches in front of him.

But then some Pharisees push their way through the crowd to get in front of Jesus. One of them throws up his arms and orders Jesus to tell the people to stop.

Jesus stays calm. "I tell you, if they are silent, you will hear the stones shout out."

The Pharisees get pushed back into the crowd, and Jesus keeps moving up the road. I watch until I can't see Jesus anymore. I can still hear the crowd shouting out their praises.

"Dad," I ask, "can we follow them and hear what he says?"

"No, Abe. There are too many people, and it's getting late. Tomorrow's another day."

"You mean we can come see him tomorrow too?"

"Yes. I promise."

I turn to Uncle Jacob. "Do you think he'll be at the temple tomorrow?"

"Absolutely!"

"Do you think he'll stay for the Passover?"

Uncle Jacob rubs his chin. "Well, if I were him, I wouldn't. The leaders are trying to figure out how to stop this whole Jesus movement. The Pharisees, Sadducees—even the priests are out to get him."

I know what they're going to do, but I'm trying hard to think like Jesus told the disciples to think. I have to stop hoping God will save Jesus. I feel angry at the ones who want to hurt him, but I don't think Jesus would want me to hate anyone. I have to stop thinking so hard. Maybe Uncle Jacob knows more, I think. So I ask.

"What will they do to Jesus?"

"Who knows? How can you stop a following like Jesus has? They almost have to lock him up in prison forever or something."

No, I know that's not how this is going to end. It's hard to hold back the panic and fear I'm feeling. I can almost hear Zag telling me to have faith in God's plan. Zag was right, and I repeat his words to myself over and over.

I'm not paying attention to the conversation now, nor where we're walking. I'm surprised when we turn the corner onto my uncle's street. It's dinner time—I can smell food cooking. I suddenly realize I'm hungry!

Aunt Sarah has dinner ready and puts a bowl of soup on the table for each of us as we wash up.

We all sit down, almost too hungry to wait for Aunt Sarah. She checks on baby Ruth, sleeping in a cradle against the wall. After Sarah sits down, we all hold hands. Uncle Jacob gives Grandpa a nod to say the blessing.

Grandpa bows his head. "Blessed are you, Lord our God, ruler of the universe, at whose word all came to be."

Uncle Jacob passes the bread. The soup is thick like stew, and hot. Uncle Jacob holds up his spoon. "I think we should just go to the Temple Mount tomorrow and wait for Jesus," he says. "He's either at Bethany or the Mount of Olives. If he comes into Jerusalem, he'll definitely show up there."

Grandpa swallows before he speaks. "Yeah, that's a good idea. We can find a quiet place to say prayers while we're there too."

After a few minutes, I stop listening to the grown-ups talk. I'm tired from the trip. I'm tired of being afraid to tell Dad about my adventure. I'm tired from standing all day waiting for Jesus. But mostly I'm tired from worrying about them hurting Jesus. Dinner was really good, but I'm done.

"May I be excused? I'm really tired. I'd like to go to bed."

"Of course, Abe," Aunt Sarah says. "Jeremiah sleeps in the back bedroom. Your bed is under the window at the top of the stairs."

"Thank you, Aunt Sarah. And thank you for dinner. It was delicious." I grab my bag and run up the stairs.

"Good night, son," Dad calls after me. "Sleep well. We have a busy day tomorrow."

I wave at the grown-ups as I disappear into my room.

I change into my nightclothes and crawl into bed. I lie on my back and watch the stars through the window. I think about our trip, about Dad not believing me. I wonder when he will. I laugh when I remember how Grandpa said maybe I saw those disciples in my dream.

I love how everyone treated Jesus when he came up that road. Jesus looked so calm riding that colt. I was glad his disciples were there to clear a path for him. I hate that those Pharisees tried to ruin it all. And then I start to think about what's going to happen to Jesus.

I don't want to think about it.

I roll over on my side and think about Zag. He's right; I have to trust God's plan. I hold my arm up to the window and give Zag a thumbs-up. I'm sure he can see it.

I pull my hand under the blanket and fall asleep.

CHAPTER 7

TURNING THE TABLES

I wake up to the sun shining down on me through the window. I can't get dressed fast enough. I race downstairs to see if Dad, Grandpa, and Uncle Jacob are ready to go. They aren't. They're sitting at the table, eating breakfast. The baby is in the cradle, and Jeremiah is playing with her.

Aunt Sarah sets a bowl of porridge on the table, then motions for me to sit and eat. "It's hot," she warns me.

"Thank you!" I sit down and scoop some up. It tastes different than Mom's, and I can't figure it out. "This is really good, Aunt Sarah," I say.

She smiles and rubs my back as she walks past me into the kitchen.

I hardly stop to breathe between mouthfuls. I scrape my bowl clean to let everyone know I'm done. Nobody is making a move to leave. Hmm . . . that porridge was so good, maybe I could ask for a little more. Just as I open my mouth to ask, Grandpa stands up.

"Well," he says, "what do you think? Are we ready to get this day started?"

Dad and Uncle Jacob stand up too. I'd rather go to the temple than have seconds on porridge. I pick up everybody's bowls and take them to the kitchen. "Thanks again, Aunt Sarah." Then out the door we go.

We walk the same route we did yesterday, except instead of turning right to go out the gate, we go straight. We climb a lot of steps, then we get to a real wide step. Grandpa, Dad, and Uncle Jacob stop, kneel, and pray.

I guess that's what we're supposed to do, so I kneel too. I pray, "Please, God, let Jesus be in the temple today. Please let me see him."

We keep climbing steps until we get to a gate. Grandpa says, "This gate is called Huldah. It's named after a woman who prophesied to King Josiah."

"I know who King Josiah was," I say, "but I don't think I've heard of Huldah before."

Uncle Jacob throws up his hands. "Here we go—another story."

I love Grandpa's stories, and I bet Uncle Jacob does too.

"Oh, this is a good story," Grandpa says. "Want to hear it, Abe?"

I plop down on the step and say, "Yes!"

Grandpa sits down too. "Josiah's grandfather, Manasseh, was the king of Judah, but"—Grandpa shakes his head—"he had to be the worst king Judah ever had. He made the people worship idols and tried to destroy every Torah in Jerusalem."

I'm shocked at that. The Torah is God's word to us! It came straight from God through Moses. And this king tried to destroy it? Wow!

"King Manasseh listened to women who predicted the future. He sacrificed children in fire and shed a lot of innocent blood. He led

God's people down a very bad road. So God let his enemies capture Manasseh and put him in prison. It was in that dark, cold, wet prison that the king repented. He asked God to save him. And, you know, God did. The king went back to Judah and got the people to worship God again."

I ask, "How does Huldah come into this?"

"Well, after Manasseh died, Josiah's father became king. He was worse than the grandfather. After only two years, the people made Josiah king when he was only eight years old."

I can't even imagine what it would be like to be so young and be a king. Josiah was way younger than me, and I seem to be too young for everything. But Grandpa's still talking.

"All the Torahs were destroyed except one. Someone had hidden it in the temple walls, but a priest named Hilkiah found it. He gave it to Josiah, and when Josiah read it, he realized they weren't following the Law of Moses at all.

"Josiah was sure God was going to punish them for that. He asked God for mercy. That's when Huldah told him a disaster would come but not until after his reign."

"What disaster?"

"Many years later, the Babylonians marched into Jerusalem and destroyed the temple. They destroyed a lot of the palaces and larger homes too. They tore down the walls around Jerusalem and took almost all the Jewish people back to Babylon to live. And that was the end of Israel and Judah."

"Wow! I love your stories, Grandpa."

Grandpa's smile shows he liked hearing that. He stands up. "Let's go find Jesus," he says.

I almost forgot we were on our way to find Jesus. Then I remember what Zag said about how God waited for the perfect time to send Jesus.

I think about the Jewish people and all the things they went through. Good things and bad things. But in the end, their faith survived it all. I feel proud of them. They're my people.

And now, Jesus is here to save the world! I jump up with everyone else, and my excitement to see Jesus rushes back.

We go through the Huldah Gate and into a tunnel that leads us to more steps. My legs are hurting already from all the steps we've climbed today.

Uncle Jacob sees the look on my face. "This will take us up into the Temple Mount, Abe," he says.

So I climb. And as soon as I step out of the tunnel into the hot sun, I forget all about my legs.

The sun almost blinds me at first. I cover my eyes and look down. The floor of the courtyard is made of flat stones. When my eyes adjust enough, I look up at the temple. It's so big and so tall and so incredibly shiny in the sun. It looks like it's made of gold.

Grandpa breaks into my thoughts. "This is the courtyard. It's open to the public. Both the Jewish people and the gentiles can be here."

The courtyard is huge. It's a long walk to go across the courtyard to the temple. The space is full of people, and it's noisy. It reminds me of the market in Bethlehem.

There are tables and tables of people selling things. Buyers are haggling about prices, but the sellers refuse to sell cheaper. They're selling sheep, goats, cattle, and oxen, all for people to offer as sacrifices in the temple. Under the tables are cages filled with birds. I take a step and realize there are animal droppings all over the flat stones. It stinks here!

Uncle Jacob tries to tell us something, but we can't hear him. He turns to face us. "This is getting worse every year. People don't want to walk around the Temple Mount to get to the Mount of Olives. Their gardens are over there—not to mention it's a shortcut when they go to Bethany. So they use the Temple Mount to get to the other side."

Uncle Jacob swings his arm around, pointing to all the sellers. "Then these people started selling stuff here during major festivals. The chief priests tax everything that's sold here. The more that's sold, the better it is for them."

Grandpa puts his hands over his ears to shut out the noise. "Let's get away from this mess and go to the men's court."

Uncle Jacob takes the lead and we follow. I can't see over the people we're pushing through to even look for Jesus.

"Let's go up here." Uncle Jacob heads up some stairs and we follow.

I know where we are. I've been here before. "We're in the men's court!" I proudly declare.

"You're right, Abe." Dad seems pleased that I remembered that.

We all stand there for a long time looking into the priest's court. Only Jewish people are allowed here, and they're here to confess their sin. We watch as they place their hands on the sacrifice they have offered.

As I stand there, I pray for Jesus. I pray for him to come to the temple today. I pray for the people to know who he is and why he came. I pray for God to help him with the sacrifice he has to make. I know God knows my heart and that I don't want Jesus to die. I tell God I'm sorry for that. I pray for God to help me have faith in his plan.

Grandpa turns and walks toward the stairs. "I think we should head down to Solomon's Porch, so we'll know when Jesus gets here. Besides, I need to sit for a bit."

We don't talk much. We're all deep in our own thoughts. No matter where we go, there are a lot of people. But then it is the Feast of Unleavened Bread and the Passover. It seems like every Jewish person must be here.

"This is Solomon's Porch, Abe," Grandpa says. "It runs the full length of the courtyard on the east side of the Temple Mount."

We walk over to the porch. It's shaded with a wood covering built on top of pillars. The ground is covered with smooth, colorful, square bricks that fit together perfectly.

Grandpa finds a place for us to sit down. I'm glad to rest, but I'd rather see Jesus. Grandpa points to the back of the temple. "You know, Abe, the most holy place is in that end of the temple. Only the high priest can go in there."

"Why?" I know why, of course—every Jewish boy does—but I want to hear Grandpa's story.

But Grandpa keeps it simple. "That's where God's presence is. Our sin keeps us from going in."

I can't help but think about God's plan. I drift off in my thoughts.

We sit there long enough for Grandpa to doze off. None of us talk—we just watch the people walking around. We're quite a ways away from those people selling stuff, but I can still hear them arguing about prices.

After a while, we hear a commotion at the front of the temple. I stand up to see what it is, and then I see him. I push Dad's shoulder. "Dad, there's Jesus! He's over there in the middle of that crowd. Can we go over?"

"Wake up, Grandpa," Dad says. "We're on the move again."

Grandpa grunts as he pushes himself up.

I don't think there can be anyone in Judah who doesn't know about Jesus. Everyone wants to see him or touch him and be healed. I wish Mom could be here. I know Jesus would heal her.

Uncle Jacob points. "Huh. Looks like he's trying to head over to the tables where they're selling. Let's make our way over there before the crowd does."

I keep my eyes on Jesus the whole way over to the tables. He isn't moving very fast because the crowd is pressing in on him. By the time he gets to the tables, we're already there, waiting.

Suddenly, Jesus lifts a table and flips it over. Everything on the table goes flying, including the coins. He walks over to another table and flips that one too.

The crowd moves back, because we're all surprised to see Jesus do that. Coins are flying everywhere. The sellers are on the ground trying to gather them up before someone else does.

Jesus flips a third table, then picks up a cord. He twists it together and then goes after the animals. He chases them out of the Temple Mount. People scatter just to get out of the way of the animals.

Jesus throws the cord down, then picks up a box of coins from another table. He holds it up and pours the coins out on the ground.

Then he says, loud enough for everyone to hear, "This is a house for prayer. But you have turned it into a marketplace. A place for robbers and thieves!"

Suddenly, the crowd is dead quiet.

Uncle Jacob whispers, with a smirk, "It's about time someone did something about that."

Jesus turns to go back toward the temple, so we follow him.

Uncle Jacob points over to some chief priests who are in a huddle, arguing with each other. He shakes his head. "I can tell they're not happy about any of this."

We keep following Jesus. He stops to heal a lame man, and then he heals a blind man. I know Mom couldn't make the trip, but I feel so guilty that she isn't here.

Some people in the crowd start singing praises like they did when he rode in on that colt yesterday. That makes the chief priests angry, and one of them almost knocks me over as they push past us. They storm up to Jesus with downright anger.

"Don't you hear what they're saying?" they scream.

Jesus calmly turns to them. "For sure you must have read, 'Praise will come out of the mouths of infants and babies' for yourself?"

The priests must know what Jesus is talking about, because it stops them dead in their tracks. Their mouths are open, but they can't seem to find words to speak.

Jesus turns and heads back toward the stairs to the Golden Gate. And then, just like that, he's gone. We all stand there staring at the steps where Jesus vanished.

"I'm telling you," Uncle Jacob says, "they're going to find one way or another to get rid of him. They do not like the attention he's getting. They are afraid of him."

Dad and Grandpa both shake their heads back and forth with sadness.

Thinking out loud, I say, "I hate that it's so hard for them to believe Jesus is the promised Messiah."

Dad is still staring at the steps where Jesus vanished. "I remember Jesus said that adults need to be more like children," he says. "I guess it's just too hard for some adults to believe like children do."

We all stand there, staring at the steps, saying nothing.

After a while, Grandpa motions for us to follow him. He says, "Abe, there's something I want you to see up here on the north side of the Temple Mount." We follow him through a gate, and he tells me, "This is the Sheep's Gate. I want to show you a pool of water back here called the Pool of Bethesda."

It's down the hill a ways. There are no steps to get down to it. Instead, there's a smooth, paved walkway slanting downward. We walk all the way down the walkway to the left. At the end, we turn and walk down another slanted walkway to the right. We end up down the hill at the same level as the pool.

"They put those walkways in," Grandpa explains, "so animals being sacrificed can get up into the Temple Mount."

That's really smart, I think. Now that we're closer, I can see the Pool of Bethesda is actually two very big pools. They're surrounded with rows of pillars and a wooden roof that shades the pools. It's just like Solomon's Porch.

"This pool is to wash the sheep before they're offered as a sacrifice," Grandpa says.

There are people lying on mats all around the pool.

"Why are they here?" I ask.

"People who are sick come here. They believe that if the pool starts to stir, the first one in gets healed."

That seems odd. "Is that true?"

"I don't really know for sure. We hear a lot of stories but can't say if they're true or not."

Uncle Jacob breaks in. "Well, I have a story for you about this pool."

We all look at Uncle Jacob and wait for him to tell his story.

"There was this paralyzed guy who came to this pool every day. Jesus saw him one day and asked if he wanted to be healed. The guy complained and asked, 'How can I be healed? I don't have anyone to help me get into the pool when it stirs.' So Jesus told him to stand up, pick up his mat, and walk. I'm telling you, this man was paralyzed his whole life. But he picked up his mat and walked away with it."

"Is that true?" Dad asks.

"Yes. But would you believe the leaders got mad at the guy for carrying his mat on the Sabbath?"

We all laugh, and still laughing, Grandpa says, "How about we head home?"

Uncle Jacob answers, "That's a great idea."

We retrace our steps up the slanted walkways and back through the Temple Mount. By now, all the sellers are gone, and it's easy to get across the courtyard. As we step into the tunnel, I wonder if Jesus ever comes this way. I look back one more time to see if Jesus is there, but he's not. We make our way down the steps, and in no time, we're home.

* * *

The day is almost over, and I want to have some time to myself. I go upstairs and fall back on my bed. I look out the window, up at the sky. I think about everything I saw on my adventure with Zag. I have to smile. Of everything I've experienced this last week, seeing Jesus is the best part of it all. I wish the chief priests and leaders would just leave him alone. Why can't they see that he's the Messiah?

I really don't want Jesus to die. But Peter felt the same way, and Jesus scolded him. I remind myself again that I must have faith in God's plan . . . but it's so hard sometimes.

Dad calls me down to dinner. I answer, "Okay," and jump up. As I come down the stairs, I can smell the food and realize I'm hungry.

Grandpa says the prayer, and I wait for the food to get passed to me.

Dad drops a spoonful of greens on his plate. He says, "Tomorrow we'll go to the temple again. But the next day, we'll do our tour with Grandpa. You okay with that, Abe?"

I start to run it through my head. Tomorrow we see Jesus, the next day go on a tour, and the next day is Passover. I realize that tomorrow could be the last time I see Jesus if he leaves Jerusalem after the Passover.

"I want to go on the tour, Dad. Really, I do. But the next day is Passover, and we won't be able to spend time at the temple. I want to see Jesus more than just tomorrow."

Dad shakes his head, and with a smile, he says, "I'm sure Jesus will stay in Jerusalem for the full eight days of Unleavened Bread. I promise, Abe, we won't go home until you see Jesus one more time after the Passover. You have my word."

I can't hold back my excitement. "Thanks, Dad!" I put some food on my plate and start eating. I don't hear much of anything else that's said at the table. All I know is I'm hungry, I'm eating, and I get to see Jesus after the Passover.

Aunt Sarah is holding the baby at the table. Everybody else gets up to go sit by the fireplace. I carry the dishes into the kitchen for Aunt Sarah, and then ask, "Can I help you clean up?"

She smiles in a way that makes me miss Mom. She says, "Thank you, Abe. But why don't you go enjoy the fire? I have to feed Ruth, and then I'll clean up the dishes."

"Okay, I will, and thank you."

I sit on the edge of the fireplace. The fire makes me warm and sleepy.

I stare into the fire, thinking of the night Jesus sat around the fire with his disciples. I could tell it was hard for Jesus to tell the disciples that he has to die. I feel sad for him.

Dad says, "Abe, you look tired. Why don't you head up to bed and get yourself a good night's rest? Tomorrow is another busy day."

"Jeremiah is already sleeping," Uncle Jacob says, "so please be quiet."

I'm happy to be alone with my thoughts, so I say, "Okay. Good night, everyone."

I go upstairs and change into my bedclothes, but instead of crawling into bed, I kneel on top of it and cross my arms on the windowsill. I look out at the sky, and I'm sure Zag is close by.

I remember Grandpa telling a story about Daniel. Daniel prayed out his window three times a day. It was illegal to pray then, and he got caught. They threw him into a lions' den.

I wonder if I have faith like Daniel's. I don't have to worry about lions. I just have to have faith in God's plan. I crawl into bed. My thoughts and the sounds from downstairs fade away.

CHAPTER 8

TRICKING JESUS

When I wake up, the only thing that matters to me is spending this day at the temple, listening to Jesus. It's practically all I think about anymore. I come downstairs and panic when I only see Aunt Sarah.

"Where is everyone?" I ask with alarm. "Did they leave already?"

Aunt Sarah smiles. "Relax, Abe. They haven't left for the Temple Mount yet. They went to get a lamb for our Passover meal. Come and sit and have some breakfast."

I sit down at the table and take a couple long breaths of relief. Aunt Sarah puts a bowl of porridge in front of me. She rubs my back like Mom does and says, "There's no hurry. Take your time eating your breakfast."

I do, and I enjoy every mouthful. "Aunt Sarah, what do you put in the porridge that makes it taste so good?"

She smiles and says, "It's a secret. But I'll tell you if you promise not to tell anyone."

"Not even Mom?" I tease. But thinking about Mom makes me sad and I lose my smile. "Dad's been making the porridge since Mom's been sick. I guess I'd have to tell him."

Aunt Sarah gives me a hug from behind. "I'll tell you what," she says. "My secret ingredient is cinnamon, and I'll send some of it home with your dad, okay?"

My smile returns. I don't think I've ever had cinnamon before. "Yeah, thanks!"

I finish eating and put my bowl in the kitchen. Aunt Sarah is sitting by the fire feeding my cousin Ruth. I go outside to watch for Dad and Grandpa and Uncle Jacob and decide to go up on the roof. It feels so high, and I can almost see across the whole valley. I look down the street and see kids playing. They're having fun kicking a big ball of rags back and forth in the street.

The hot sun feels good. I wave back at some people sitting on a roof a few houses down. It feels like it's taking forever, and I'm wondering how far they had to go for the lamb. I walk down the stairs to the street to wait. Finally, I see them coming. Uncle Jacob is carrying Jeremiah. Grandpa is holding a rope that's tied around a lamb's neck. That poor lamb has to run just to keep up with them. They're all tall and walk with long strides.

The kids in the street run over to play with the lamb. A neighbor comes out of a house and picks it up. The men are busy talking. I stand up to wait for them to come home. Finally they see me, and that makes them say goodbye.

Uncle Jacob comes up the street, saying to me, "You look like you're ready to go."

"I sure am."

Uncle Jacob brings Jeremiah into the house.

We're leaving later than I wanted to, but it's okay. We're on our way now. We stop to pray at that big flat step again and then go through the gate. We climb the steps in the tunnel and come out into the courtyard. I squint my eyes in the sun as I look for him.

"There he is! He's in the middle of that crowd!"

Jesus is trying to get to the temple, but it's a slow walk because of all the people around him. We finally catch up to him just as some chief priests and elders stop him. One of them demands, "Who gave you the authority to do what you're doing?"

Jesus pauses for a moment, then says, "I will ask you one thing. If you answer me, then I'll answer you."

They don't know what to say to that, so they wait for Jesus to ask his question.

"The baptism of John," he says. "Was that from heaven or man?"

They look confused and don't say anything.

"Answer me," Jesus urges.

It seems like a simple question to me, but the chief priests and elders back away from Jesus and huddle into a group. They're arguing with each other. They're so upset, they get loud enough for us to hear.

"Look," one elder says, "we can't say heaven. Jesus will ask why we didn't believe John."

"Well, we can't say man. Too many people liked John, and they'll turn against us."

They come out of their huddle and reluctantly admit, "We don't know."

Jesus smiles and says, "Then I can't answer your question either." Jesus turns to the crowd and starts telling a story.

"A man plants a vineyard. He hires a farmer to take care of the crop."

It's a long story, and I don't understand it, but the chief priests sure do. It makes them so mad, they walk away. I try not to laugh as I watch them walk. Their fancy robes are filling with air and flapping behind them.

Some Pharisees are there watching them walk away too. They must decide it's their turn to pick on Jesus, because now they interrupt him. "Is it lawful for the Jewish people to pay tax to Caesar or not?"

Jesus doesn't answer them, so they ask louder.

"Should we or shouldn't we pay tax to Caesar?"

I hate that they're being so mean and rude to Jesus.

Dad gives Uncle Jacob a tap on his arm, "They're asking trick questions."

"Yeah," he answers back. "It's like they're trying to test Jesus or catch him saying something wrong."

It doesn't work, because Jesus sees right through it. "You hypocrites," he says. "Why are you trying to test me or trick me? Give me a coin and let me see it."

The Pharisees hand Jesus a coin.

He looks at it, then holds it up so the crowd can see it. "Whose head is this on the coin?" he asks.

Without even looking at the coin, the crowd answers. "The emperor's."

Jesus hands the coin back and says, "Give to the emperor what belongs to the emperor. Give to God what belongs to God."

Uncle Jacob smiles and whispers, "That'll shut them up."

But then some Sadducees break through the crowd and start badgering him.

"Moses said if a man dies and has no children, his brother should marry the widow. He should have children for his brother. But let's say there are seven brothers, and they all die with no children. Whose wife will she be in the resurrection?"

That makes Grandpa mad. "The Sadducees don't even believe in the resurrection," he grumbles. "Why would they even ask Jesus that question?"

"They're trying to trick him too," Dad says.

But Jesus answers them saying, "They won't marry or be given in marriage. They'll be like angels in heaven."

I can't help but think of Zag and wonder if he's listening.

"God is the God of the living, not the dead," Jesus says.

Grandpa shakes his head and grins. "Boy! I could listen to Jesus teach all day."

All three of us murmur back our agreement. The whole crowd—except the leaders, of course—seems to be amazed with Jesus.

And then another Pharisee interrupts with his question. "Which law is the greatest?"

I know they're still trying to trick Jesus, but we're all hanging onto every word he says. I look back at Jesus in time to see him smile. I think he's been waiting for that question all day.

He looks at us in the crowd with love and compassion. Then he puts both hands on his heart and answers that question. "The greatest commandment is to love the Lord your God with all your heart. Love Him with all your soul." Jesus points a finger to his temple. "Love Him with all your mind. This is the greatest law." Jesus keeps one hand on his heart, but he's not done. He holds up two fingers as he continues. "The second greatest law is this: You should love your neighbor like you love yourself."

Jesus looks across the crowd and says, "No other law is greater than these two."

A scribe agrees. "You're right, teacher. Those two laws are even more important than any burnt offering or sacrifice."

Jesus looks at the scribe with love and says, "You are very close to understanding the kingdom of God."

Uncle Jacob notices the few chief priests, scribes, and Pharisees remaining are starting to walk away. "Look!" he says. "They're all leaving. I guess they don't have any more questions."

Jesus turns back to the crowd. "Watch out for the ones who walk around in fancy long robes and want to be noticed in public places. And the ones who want the best seats in the synagogues and at banquets. Yes, they stun you with their long prayers, but they do it for the sake of appearance. These same people won't hesitate to take a widow's house from her."

Jesus walks toward the temple, and we all follow him. Jesus stops, but Grandpa points to a room just inside the temple. "Let's go in there," he says. "I need to sit for a while."

I want to stay outside and listen to Jesus, but I know better than to ask. I can hear Jesus talking, but I can't hear what he's saying.

Grandpa points at the wall. "Hey, Abe, see those pillars along that wall?"

I look, and every pillar has a container mounted on it shaped like a big trumpet. "Yes."

"Those are treasure boxes mounted on the pillars. That's where people pay their tithes to the temple."

I count thirteen of them. There's a steady flow of people coming in to drop coins in the boxes. This is interesting. Some people drop their coins quietly. Some drop them quickly. A few make a big thing about how many coins they drop in. I can tell who's rich by the way they're dressed and how many coins they drop in.

I'm so absorbed with watching these people drop coins in the treasure boxes that I forget Jesus is just outside the door. Grandpa nods off and is sleeping hard.

Suddenly, Dad nudges me. Jesus is coming in with his disciples. They sit down almost next to us, and for some reason, the crowd hasn't followed him in.

I can't believe we're here by ourselves with Jesus! I squeeze my eyes shut and say a quick *thank you* to God. Jesus and his friends seem to be taking a rest from the crowd, just like us. Together, we watch people come in and drop coins in the boxes.

An old lady catches my eye, and then I see Jesus is watching her too. She's bent over and is using a stick to keep her balance. Slowly, she shuffles her way toward a treasure box. She's wearing a worn-out brown dress that drags on the ground behind her. Her head scarf is thin, and a few wisps of stringy gray hair are sneaking out from under it. She looks like she's had a very hard life, and I feel bad for her.

She pulls a rag from her waist sash and draws out two coins. It's so quiet in the room now that we hear each of her coins drop into the treasure box. She pushes the rag back into her sash and shuffles out the door. No one says a word, but I'm sure we're all thinking about that old lady.

Then Jesus says, "I tell you, this poor widow has put in more than anyone."

Now, I watched a lot of people drop way more than she did into that treasure box. The way Dad and even the disciples are looking at Jesus, I think everybody else is thinking the same thing too. So Jesus continues.

"All the others gave small portions of what they have. Those two coins were all she had to live on."

I love the way Jesus thinks. I don't know how anybody can't love him.

Jesus stands up to leave. Right away, I'm making faces at Dad, motioning that I want to follow him, but Dad shakes his head no. The disciples follow Jesus out of the temple, and we sit there a few minutes longer. Finally, Grandpa stretches and stands up. It's time to go.

I step out of the temple and look around for Jesus, but I don't see him anywhere. We walk across the long courtyard. I do a final scan before I go down the steps into the tunnel. Jesus is gone.

The way home is so familiar, I don't really pay attention to the turns anymore. Before I know it, we're walking up to Uncle Jacob's house, and I can smell dinner cooking. My stomach growls loudly, reminding me that we didn't make it home for lunch.

Aunt Sarah tells us dinner will be ready in fifteen minutes, so I excuse myself and go upstairs to lie on my bed for some alone time.

I can't help but think about how all those leaders tried to trick Jesus. Jesus liked what that one scribe said, though. I wonder what it would be like to be a scribe. All they do is write the Torah over and over, so we have more copies of it. I'm glad they do that, but I don't think I could. My heart fills with funny emotions when I think about that old lady and about what Jesus said. He really can see what's in our hearts.

My alone time is over when Dad calls me to come eat. I run downstairs, wash my hands, and am the last one to the table. Grandpa starts the blessing as soon as I sit.

Aunt Sarah is a good cook. She hasn't cooked anything I don't like. Normally we have wheat bread, but tonight she's made unleavened flatbread. I watch Uncle Jacob lay one piece on his plate and pour stew over it. It looks good, and everybody does the same thing. The pieces are big, so I only take half of one. I take a bite and, with food still in my mouth, say, "This is *really* good!"

Aunt Sarah smiles. "I thought you would like it, Abe."

Over dinner, we tell Aunt Sarah about our day. Grandpa tells her about the lady and the two coins. I kind of get lost in the deliciousness of the food and don't pay close attention to Grandpa's story, until . . .

"The leaders tried really hard to trick Jesus with their questions today." Uncle Jacob has my full attention.

Dad agrees. "Maybe it's part of their plot to do away with Jesus."

"It's obvious they don't like Jesus and feel threatened by him."

Why does everything have to end up being about something bad happening to Jesus? I almost forgot that Jesus has to die. I almost had one full day I didn't think about that. Now I can't get it out of my head. Thinking about it is going to ruin the whole day.

I help Aunt Sarah clear the table, then I make myself comfortable by the fire.

Dad says something about paying taxes, and Uncle Jacob tells him about some city tax he has to pay for his house. Grandpa repeats the argument he had with the officers at the gate.

They're talking about everything except Jesus. I don't want to hear it, so I excuse myself and go upstairs.

I crawl into bed, look out the window at the stars, and relive the whole day in my head. I remember the story Jesus told that made the chief priests so mad. I still don't understand that one, but I do love the answer Jesus gave about the coin and paying Caesar.

I remember what Jesus said about the two greatest laws. I'll have to remember to tell Mom and Adam that. I remember that widow and her two coins. I could tell Jesus loved her and what she did.

I run out of good things to think about. I start to think about what Jesus said about being killed. I hate thinking about that.

Jesus did say he'll rise on the third day, but I'm not sure what that means. Zag's voice whispers through my memories. *Have faith in God's plan.* I feel a little better.

My thoughts and dreams blend together. I don't know when, but I fall asleep.

CHAPTER 9

THE TOUR

Breakfast is porridge again, but I love Aunt Sarah's porridge. Jeremiah is standing next to Uncle Jacob, who has Ruth on his shoulder. He's patting her back and trying to make her burp. Uncle Jacob grins at me.

"Well, good morning, Abe. You got your walking shoes on? We're going to do a lot of walking today."

I nod because my mouth is crammed full of porridge.

Dad raises an eyebrow at me. "Slow down, son," he says. "We're in no hurry."

I can't wait to get started on our tour. "What are we going to see, Grandpa?" I ask.

"Well, I thought we'd go see the Hippodrome first."

"The *what*?"

He laughs. "It's easier to show you than explain it. After that I'll show you how King David was able to conquer Jerusalem. Then we'll check out some of the palaces here."

The baby burps and Jeremiah jumps back. "Eww! Ruthie spit up on Dad."

Uncle Jacob hands the baby to Aunt Sarah. "Yup," he says. "Got to change clothes before we go." He disappears into the bedroom.

By the time he comes back, I'm scraping up my last mouthful of porridge. I put my bowl in the kitchen and thank Aunt Sarah for breakfast.

She hands Uncle Jacob a bag with our lunch. We say our goodbyes and head out the door. We walk straight north toward the Temple Mount. With almost too much excitement, I ask Grandpa, "Are we going back to the temple?"

"No," he answers. "I told you, we're going to the Hippodrome. It's a big arena where people go to be entertained."

Before he can finish getting the words out, I see it. It's a tall, long, enormous building. There are about thirty steps all around it leading up to walls of pillars. The pillars are tall, with round arches between them at the top. The corners have round towers with small windows.

We climb about halfway up the steps until Grandpa points to an opening. "Let's use that entrance," he says.

We go inside, and the first thing I notice is there's no roof. There are wide steps all around the inside, from the ground up to the pillars. I can picture thousands of people sitting on the steps to watch whatever happens here.

At one end of the arena, two big wooden doors are at ground level. In the middle of the arena is a narrow, long platform. There's a wide, oval, dirt track all around it. We go down a few steps, and Grandpa sits down. He pats the stone next to him for me to sit.

Grandpa sweeps his arm around in front of us and I look where he points. "King Herod built this for chariot races," he says. "I don't know if you've ever seen a chariot, Abe. It's a small, two-wheeled wagon pulled by four horses. Soldiers use them in battles."

I remember the chariots at the Red Sea, racing through those walls of water. I was so scared when I saw those chariots coming at me. I shiver just thinking about it.

Grandpa looks at me. "Are you cold, Abe?"

"I think it's just the cold, hard stone I'm sitting on. How can anyone sit here for very long?"

"I think a better question is, how can anyone sit here and watch those races? They were dangerous. Men and horses were always getting killed. Most Jewish people hated what went on in this arena." Grandpa stops and shakes his head in disgust. "But as much as they said they hated it, this place was always full of people wanting to watch. Isn't that right, Jacob?"

"You're right. People seem to love watching stuff like that."

We all sit in silence trying to imagine the chariot races and the noise of the crowds. Grandpa gives me a nudge and says, "The Jewish leaders complained a lot."

Uncle Jacob adds, "But that didn't stop the games."

"And it didn't stop the people from coming to see them either," Grandpa says.

"But Herod is dead now," I say. "Why can't they just tear all this down and get rid of it?"

Uncle Jacob stands up. "His son, Herod Antipas, rules in Galilee. He comes here a lot. He's not nearly as bad as Herod was, but the leaders are still afraid of him."

"We live out in the country, Abe," Dad says. "We don't have the Roman soldiers or a governor close by to remind us they're in control. For people living in Jerusalem, it's very real and sometimes very hard. Maybe someday Jerusalem will go back to being a city for the Jewish people, a city where we'll have the freedom to live like we want." He stands up and adds, "But that is not today."

Dad helps Grandpa stand up from the low step. We're ready to go.

"Okay." Grandpa starts the trek out of the Hippodrome. "Let's head south, and I'll show you how King David conquered this city."

We go out the door and down the stairs to the street. We head to the south end of the city. It's mostly uphill, so our walk is a little slower. The streets are all narrow and lined with houses. It's hard to tell where one house ends and another starts. Two homes share one wall. I'm not sure how anyone can talk without their neighbor hearing.

Uncle Jacob points to the long row of homes. He says, "The people living in this section are the poorest people in Jerusalem. They don't own their homes—they pay to live here. Most of these houses have two or more families living in them."

I watch the women share buckets of water for washing clothes. There are kids playing everywhere. It's noisy. We reach a short wall on the edge of the hill.

"Before Jerusalem was Jerusalem," Grandpa says, "it was the city of Jebus. It had walls all around it, and the king knew they were safe. But they had to go outside the walls to get water."

He leans over the short wall and points to the bottom of the hill. "See that spring down there?"

I look and nod yes.

"That's called the Gihon Spring, and that's where they had to go to get their water. The king had the people dig a long tunnel through the earth and connect it to that spring."

I'm amazed they could dig a tunnel so far down into the ground. I say, "That was smart."

Grandpa smiles. "Smart, but not so smart. King David used that tunnel to get inside the walls and take the city. He named the city Jerusalem, and it became the capital of Judah."

"I love your stories, Grandpa." I reach over and give him a quick hug before I pull away from the edge of the wall. I turn and look up the street. There's a big pool of water up there. "Look at that!" And I head over to see it.

Everybody heads toward the pool. I'm close enough now to see it has steps all around it, going down into the pool. The water is so clear, I can see the bottom, and it's deep.

"This is the Pool of Siloam," Grandpa tells me. "King Hezekiah built it so the city would have a good source of water. That is, in case enemies decided to camp outside the gates."

"Oh!" Uncle Jacob interrupts. "Okay, Abe. Now *I* have a story to tell. You're gonna like this one!"

Grandpa looks at Uncle Jacob and smiles. He's ready to listen too.

"There's this blind guy who used to go to the Temple Mount every day to beg for money, until one day I saw him, and it was obvious he could see where he was going. So I asked him what was going on—I knew he was blind, so what happened? How could he see now?

"He tells me about a man who scooped up some dirt and spit in it to make mud. Then the man rubbed the mud over his eyes and told him to go wash in the Pool of Siloam. He did what the man told him to do, and when he opened his eyes, he could see!"

I'm pretty sure I know, but I ask anyway. "Was it Jesus who put the mud on his eyes?"

"I asked him, and he didn't know. But it had to be Jesus. He was here in Jerusalem when it happened."

I shake my head. All I can say is, "Wow."

"Wow is right," Grandpa says. Then he turns back toward the street. We're on the move again.

"What's next on our tour, Grandpa?" I ask.

"Mmm . . . how about we go see the high priest's palace?"

"Oh, great!" Uncle Jacob says. "We're off to see Caiaphas."

Just hearing the name *Caiaphas* takes the good out of the moment. Zag told me Caiaphas is Jesus's biggest enemy. He's trying to convince the leaders that Jesus needs to die for the people. That it's the only way to save the nation.

But Jesus isn't trying to destroy the nation. He came to save us! Why can't they understand that? My stomach starts to knot up.

Suddenly, Uncle Jacob stops us. "Let's head up this street. There's a cutover two blocks up."

I'm not paying attention to where we're going until I glance down a side street and see two of Jesus's disciples. They're coming out of a big, two-story building.

Who cares about Caiaphas? I grab Dad's arm. "Dad, look! Those two men are Jesus's disciples. They just came out of that building."

Before Dad can answer, Grandpa says, "You're right, Abe. I saw them with Jesus at the Temple Mount."

"Hmm," says Uncle Jacob. "I wonder what business they have here?"

Grandpa rubs his chin. "Well, it is the day before Passover. Maybe they're looking for a place to celebrate with Jesus."

Just the thought of knowing where Jesus might celebrate Passover made me perk up. I turn to look at Dad, but Dad already knows what I'm thinking.

"No, Abe. We are not going to chase after Jesus on Passover. We'll see him after."

Uncle Jacob laughs. "You know your dad is right, don't you?"

I'm disappointed, but I smile as I answer. "Yeah, I guess so."

Uncle Jacob points ahead of us. "We're coming into the wealthy district where the rich people live. I probably don't have to tell you that—look at how things have changed. Look at the width of the streets and the size of the houses."

Oh, he's right. The streets are wider and very straight. The houses are so clean and white that the sun's glare off them almost hurts my eyes. These houses aren't like anything I've ever seen before. They have lots of space between them. They have pools and gardens with colorful flowers. I'm sure Mom would love these flowers.

I wonder what kind of people can afford to live here. Every house I pass seems to be better than the house next to it in some way. We make a turn, and there's a big building in the middle of a wide courtyard. There's another one in the back of the courtyard.

Grandpa points to the one in front and says, "That's the council building." He motions for us to follow him. "Come on. We're allowed to go into the courtyard."

The council building has ten long steps leading up to two big doors. "The Sanhedrin meets here," Grandpa says. "It's also used by special councils who investigate things for the leaders."

This courtyard is huge, spanning the width of the property. There are three stone fire pits.

Uncle Jacob says, "When the Sanhedrin holds trials, you will always see people out here. These people are here waiting to be heard or to testify or to hear their verdict. The Sanhedrin was kind enough to put these fire pits in the courtyard so people can stay warm while they wait."

I look down into one of the round fire pits. It's half full of stinky, cold, black ashes. The stones are sealed with hard clay. It makes me think back to the mud and hay mixture in Egypt. The pits are tall enough for people to hold their hands over the fire and get warm. I almost wish there was a fire in one of them now, because I feel a little chilly.

Grandpa motions for us to follow him. We go through two columns of pillars to another courtyard in the back. And *another* huge building.

"That's the palace where Caiaphas lives," Grandpa says.

It's big and has carved stone figures on the corners of the roof. There's a walk-out patio on the second floor. It's protected with small stone pillars to keep someone from falling off. Wide steps lead up to two large wooden doors with black hinges.

Why does a priest have such a fancy palace as this? I wonder.

"I thought the priests lived on the Temple Mount next to the temple?"

"They used to," Uncle Jacob answers, "but I guess power changes people. Caiaphas wasn't even in line to be the high priest, but a Roman governor gave him the title."

I remember Zag telling me that. "Is he still the Roman governor?"

"No." Uncle Jacob says. "Pontius Pilate is the governor now. We never did find out why he appointed Caiaphas to be the high priest. The Jewish leaders tried to fight it, but they couldn't change that decision. Rome dictates and we obey. Pilate isn't much better than the last one."

He shakes his head in disgust. "I know one thing for sure. Caiaphas being the high priest is bad for Jesus."

"Why?"

"Well, the chief priests and Pharisees formed a council to investigate Jesus. They're all worried because the people think Jesus is the promised Messiah."

"But he *is* the promised Messiah," I say.

"Yeah." Uncle Jacob hesitates. "But to them, it's just a rumor. They're afraid if Rome hears that rumor, they'll lose their positions of power. Or worse, they're afraid Rome will take away our status of being a Jewish nation. The council didn't know what to do, so they went to Caiaphas for advice."

The knot in my stomach gets tighter. I know the answer, but I still ask, "What did Caiaphas tell them to do?"

"He said he had a vision about Jesus. He says Jesus will die for the nation."

Dad and Grandpa stare at Uncle Jacob in disbelief.

"But he also said God will gather his children and make them a nation again." He shrugs his shoulders. "Who knows if the vision is real or not? I don't think it is. But the council believes it. I hear they're plotting to kill Jesus."

Grandpa shakes his head. "They can't! We have no Jewish laws that would allow them to kill Jesus."

I hate the thought of Jesus being killed, but I know the price to save us from our sin is Jesus's life. Jesus said so himself. I have to have faith that God already knows—and that he already *has*—what it will take to make that plan work.

I realize nobody's talking. I guess they're all trying to figure out how this is going to end up. Same as me. I break the silence.

"Grandpa, is it possible that Caiaphas is part of God's plan to save the world through Jesus?"

My question has startled all three of them. Grandpa puts his arm around my shoulders. "Abraham, Abraham! Why do you ask such difficult questions?" Then, pulling me with him as he starts walking out, he says, "Everything will be fine. We have no laws that allow them to kill Jesus. Not even Caiaphas."

"Grandpa's right, Abe." But it doesn't sound like Dad believes it.

We come around to the front courtyard. A disciple is coming out of the council building! I break free of Grandpa's hold.

"Look! That's one of Jesus's disciples. Why is he here?"

He's running and disappears quickly down the street.

"You're right again," Grandpa says. "That *was* one of his disciples. Why would he be here?"

"His coming here . . . that can't be good." Uncle Jacob looks worried.

None of us want to think about that, but we do anyway. We walk down the steps and make a left turn into the street.

I break the silence again. "Where are we going next, Grandpa?"

"We're going to see Herod's palace. It's on the west side of Jerusalem."

We walk up wide streets with more of those big fancy houses. I'm still thinking about that disciple. Two turns later, we walk out onto a street filled with shops. I forget about the disciple because I don't want to miss a thing.

This place is noisy and smells like a barn. Both sides of the street are lined with lambs, goats, oxen, and birds. Everyone seems to be talking at the same time, arguing about prices.

"This is the market," Uncle Jacob says. "They keep the animals on this end. But just a little ways up, you'll see fruits, vegetables, cloth, and all kinds of things." Uncle Jacob waves his hand in the air. "The market goes down this street for quite a ways. Herod's palace is on the left, about halfway through the market."

"This kind of reminds me of the courtyard at the Temple Mount," I say.

Uncle Jacob laughs. "Not anymore. Not if Jesus has anything to say about it."

"Watch where you step," Dad says, pointing to some animal droppings on the street.

I try to, but I don't want to miss anything.

We make it past the animals to the weavers and pottery makers. Then there are carpenters with furniture and bakers with fresh bread. We walk past metalworkers, tailors, and women dyeing cloth. I stop at a table and touch some bright, shiny blue cloth. Dad tells me it's silk. I pinch the cloth and rub it together. It feels slippery. I don't think Mom would like it.

Dad keeps us moving through the market. Suddenly, I get a whiff of something sweet. Dad points to a table across the street laden with small, clear bottles.

"That's what they call perfume," he says. "Rich women wear it, but I'm not sure why. I'd be afraid it would attract bees."

I laugh just thinking about that.

Oh, we've found the food area. The tables are heaped with fruit, olives, fish, and vegetables. Some tables are set up for sitting and eating. Fish, bread, soup. Across the street there are tables full of desserts. It all looks so good. I'm starting to feel hungry.

Grandpa looks back at me and says, "It makes you hungry, doesn't it?"

I hold my stomach and nod a big yes.

He laughs and says, "We'll eat our lunch when we get to Herod's palace. It's right up there, not far."

Just a little farther, it looks like the market ends. Uncle Jacob points up the street. "The market ends on this side of the palace and starts up again on the other side."

I see what must be the palace on the left. It's so big, it almost looks like a village inside of Jerusalem. It's built on a flat mound, about as high up as I am tall. A wall of posts surrounds it, except in the back. It ends at the west wall of the city.

We keep walking until we come to the entrance. There's a big building in the middle and two other buildings, one on the left and one on the right.

Grandpa spreads his arms wide. "This is Herod's palace, Abe. Or, I should say, palaces. He built a palace on each end of the property." Grandpa points to the palace on the left and says, "That one was for his guests. The one to the right was for himself. They both have living areas, bedrooms, baths, and banquet halls. Herod called them Agrippa and Caesar."

Caiaphas's palace is almost small compared to these buildings.

Grandpa points at the center building. "Herod used that one for parties and to entertain."

"Pontius Pilate uses that building for a courtroom," Uncle Jacob adds. "He alone decides if someone is guilty or innocent. I wouldn't want him deciding my trial if I ever had to have one."

These are the biggest buildings I've ever seen, other than the Temple Mount. But then, I guess that building I saw in Egypt was pretty huge too.

"Pilate stays in Herod's palace on the right," Uncle Jacob says. "His soldiers stay in the guest palace on the left."

Grandpa starts up the steps, and we follow him. We go through the entrance into a courtyard so wide it feels like a field. The ground is covered with thick green grass and walkways made of flat, perfectly fit tiles. A walkway leads to a pond in the center of the courtyard. The walkway splits and goes around the pond. It continues like a wide street all the way back to the entrance of the center building.

We sit down on a bench in front of the pond. I turn around to look at the statue of a man in the middle of the pond. He's short and fat, wears a long robe, and has on a lot of jewelry. There's a crown on his head, so it has to be King Herod. But I check anyway.

"Is that a statue of Herod?"

Grandpa doesn't even turn to look. Instead he grunts, "Yeah, that's him."

I turn my back to Herod and look out across the courtyard.

"What do you say we eat our lunch here?" Grandpa suggests.

"Yeah," Uncle Jacob says. "I'm hungry after walking through that market." He pulls the bread out of the bag and breaks off a chunk for each of us. It's the unleavened bread we had last night.

I chew on my bread while I look out at the trees and flowers. Thick green bushes are trimmed in all different shapes. Short bushes line the edges of the walkways. Little water canals flow through the gardens and bushes. The tiled walkways are so clean you could probably eat off them.

Uncle Jacob breaks off more bread and says, "Pontius Pilate refuses to call this Herod's palace. He calls it the Praetorium, because that's what the palace and head office in Rome is called. Anyone else want more bread?"

Grandpa and Dad both take more. I take a bite off my piece and shake my head no. We sit there for so long that Grandpa nods off. We let him sleep.

While Grandpa naps, we watch the Roman soldiers come and go. We hear a commotion in the street and look to see what it is. Even Grandpa wakes up. About six soldiers come into the courtyard, dragging a man who is fighting to get away. A woman is behind them, crying and pleading. "Please don't. He's innocent. Please."

We don't move but watch them disappear off to the side where the soldiers are staying. Uncle Jacob shakes his head.

"It's never good when they take you back there. They tie you to a post and whip you with some nasty whips. It's Rome's way of punishing someone. Not everyone survives that punishment. It's brutal."

I remember the whippings the Hebrews got when they didn't work hard enough or move fast enough for their guards. All of a sudden, I don't want to be here anymore.

It's like Grandpa can tell what I'm thinking. He gets up and says, "I think it's time to move on to our next place."

I jump up with him. "Where is that, Grandpa?"

"To the Hasmonean palace."

* * *

We walk out of the courtyard, down the steps, and turn left. The market starts up again with more shops. We take our time and stop to look at the things for sale. There are tables full of gold and silver jewelry. There are all kinds of ivory carvings and shiny colorful stones.

I smell something burning, and Dad says, "That's incense. Normally it's burned in the temple, but some people buy it to burn in their houses."

There's a woman weaving threads on a wooden loom ahead of us. I can't help but stop and admire it. It looks like a painting, but it's cloth.

Grandpa says, "That's what you call a tapestry. She weaves with different-colored threads to make a picture."

The lady motions for me to come closer. "This tapestry will have thousands of stitches when I'm done," she says. "I have to be very careful to use the right color for every stitch I make. The first stitch is just as important as the last one."

This seems so complicated. "How do you know what color to use for each stitch?"

She smiles and says, "It's easy, because I know what the picture is going to look like when it's done."

It's only half done, but I can tell it's going to be beautiful. I tell her that, and she smiles as we walk away.

We pass tables full of fruits and vegetables that I've never seen before. There are people shopping who don't look like they should be here.

I ask about that, and Grandpa tells me, "They're slaves. They belong to wealthy people on this side of town. You can tell because they're dressed like poor people, but they buy stuff most of us can't afford."

Uncle Jacob pokes me. "Hey, Abe, here's something you might not know. Did you know that the law for a slave is whatever his owner tells him to do?"

Oh, I don't like that. I don't like calling them slaves either. They're people like us. I feel sorry for them. I ask, "Do they ever see their families?"

Uncle Jacob answers. "Yes, but not very often."

The market stops and the street narrows. Now there are regular homes like Uncle Jacob's. Just as we come to a right turn, I look out and see a hill outside of the wall. It has tall poles in the ground, and it looks bare and creepy.

"Uncle Jacob! What is that place over there?"

Everyone stops to look. "They call that Golgotha. It means the place of the skull."

"Why do they call it that?"

Uncle Jacob shakes his head. "It's a place for criminals who are sentenced to death. The Romans take them to that hill and nail them to a cross. It's a horrible death."

Just thinking about it makes me feel sick.

"The Romans say they use that hill because the tombs are right there. I think they use it because it's next to the road. They want everyone to see and be afraid of them."

I don't know how anyone can be so cruel to anybody, no matter what they've done.

We keep walking, but I can't get that hill out of my head. I realize we're walking toward the Temple Mount again, and I wonder if Jesus will be there. But then I see the palace.

"Is that it, Grandpa? The Hasmonean one?"

"It sure is," he answers. "Built by the Jewish family that got us our nation back."

I can tell Grandpa is proud of the Hasmonean family.

This palace is long and high. It must be at least two levels. In the middle of the building, there's a platform way up on the second floor. There are tall, round towers at each end of the palace. It isn't as big and fancy as Herod's place, but I'm still impressed.

Grandpa points to the platform halfway up. "That's where our kings used to make speeches to the people. Everyone would gather in this courtyard where we're standing. Herod Antipas owns it now and stays here whenever he's in town."

"He's here now," Uncle Jacob adds. "He always comes here for the Passover."

Grandpa puts his hands behind him and stretches backward. He takes a deep breath. As he exhales, he says, "I think we did too much walking today. I need a rest . . . but where?"

Uncle Jacob grins at me. "I know just the place to sit and rest. Abe. What do you say we go to the Temple Mount and see if our friend is there?"

I say yes before he's even done talking.

Grandpa laughs and leads us around the corner to more steps that he says will take us up onto the Temple Mount. After walking all day, every step hurts Grandpa, but he doesn't complain. I'm sure Dad and Uncle Jacob are tired too. We take our last step up onto the Temple Mount and it puts us at the back end of the temple.

I scan the crowd, looking for Jesus, but he's nowhere to be found.

Dad sees the disappointment on my face and gives me a hug. "Don't worry, Abe. I promise you'll see Jesus before we go home."

A little pressure lifts from my chest. I look over at the north end of the Temple Mount. Way up on a hill just inside the wall is a building that looks like a fortress. Guard towers are located on each corner. Soldiers stand there, looking down into the Temple Mount.

Grandpa sees me looking at it. "That's for the Roman soldiers. It's called the Fortress of Antonia, named after a ruler in Rome. The soldiers in the towers keep an eye on the Temple Mount to make sure there's order." He shakes his head in disgust. "This fortress is just another reminder that Rome has power over us."

I walk back over to the steps where we came up. I look out at Herod's palace and the market. I can't help but see that hill. "Look, Grandpa," I say. "The people who hang on those poles over on that hill can look over here and see the temple."

Grandpa walks over to look. "You're right, they can." He looks sad. He turns around. "I think I'm ready to head home. How about you, Abe?"

I think about Jesus and wish I could have seen him here in the temple today. It's not that I don't appreciate Grandpa showing me so many important places around Jerusalem. I just would like to have seen Jesus too. But Grandpa's right.

I turn to him with a smile. "Yes, it's time to head home."

We walk across the courtyard to the tunnel that takes us out the Huldah Gate. It doesn't take long to go down all the steps. A few turns later, we're home.

Dinner is waiting for us. We wash, then sit down at the table to eat. We're all hungry but wait for Grandpa to pray.

"Blessed are you, Lord our God, King of the universe, that by whose word all things came to be."

We all eat too fast. I'm tired, and I want to go to bed, but Grandpa stops me to say a prayer before we leave the table. Without thinking, I head for the stairs.

"It's Passover," Grandpa reminds me. "We have to put a light in every corner of the house, and we have to make sure there's no leaven here."

Jeremiah gets excited and asks, "Can I help, Grandpa?"

"Yes, of course, Jeremiah. We all have to search."

I know what that means. Leaven can be in bread or cakes. Anything that's been fermented with yeast must be removed from the house. We search the whole house for it—even for crumbs in our pockets! It's something all Jewish people do the night before Passover to remember how God saved the Hebrews.

As I search, I'm thinking. It was clever for the Hebrews to call it Passover. It was the blood of a sacrificed lamb on their doorposts that saved the Hebrews that night. The Angel of Death passed over every home that had that blood on the door.

Hmm . . . the blood of a sacrifice covers our sins, and the blood on the doorposts saved the Hebrews. I hadn't really given that much thought before.

This Passover has so much more meaning because I saw the Hebrews as slaves in Egypt. I know what God saved them from. I smile to myself and think about how I barely escaped through the Red Sea. That would be a fun story to tell, but I can't.

Finally, everyone is satisfied that there's no leaven in the house, and we all go to bed. I sleep so hard I don't even remember having dreams.

CHAPTER 10

THE PASSOVER

I wake up and the sun is just coming up. It's the day of Passover, and that gets me excited. I get dressed and go downstairs. I'm hoping I'm not too late to go with Dad to the temple to sacrifice our lamb. I see that baby Ruth is in her cradle sleeping. Dad, Grandpa, and Uncle Jacob are at the table having breakfast. Jeremiah must still be sleeping.

Aunt Sarah puts a bowl of porridge on the table for me. "Sorry, Abe. Same as yesterday and the day before, I know."

I grab my spoon and smile. "That's okay. I love your porridge."

Dad finishes swallowing a mouthful of porridge. "You want to go with us to the temple, Abe?"

"Yes!" I answer. This yes feels different than a yes to go see Jesus. Sacrificing a lamb is such a sacred thing. It means redemption from our sins. It means the Hebrews being redeemed from Egypt's slavery. It's something I get to be a part of only when we come to Jerusalem.

A big pot of water is steaming on the stove, almost ready to boil. Uncle Jacob walks over to check it. "When we get back, we'll all help with the cleaning and preparations, Sarah. Don't try to do it all yourself."

"Of course," Aunt Sarah answers. "I'm happy to have the help."

I finish my breakfast and run to follow them out the door. Uncle Jacob's neighbor is waiting for us down the street with the lamb Uncle Jacob got the other day. The walk to the temple goes quick. There are a lot of people coming with lambs to be sacrificed for the Passover.

"This way." Uncle Jacob leads us to the priests' court. Today there are a lot of priests in the court and they're all dressed in bright scarlet robes. I watch as the people each make their sacrifice while the priest holds a cup to catch the blood. Then they pass the blood to other priests, who pour it out on the altar.

When it's our turn to offer our sacrifice, we all follow Uncle Jacob and his neighbor. Together they make the sacrifice. I watch as the priest catches the blood and passes it on to the other priest, who slowly pours it on the altar.

I don't understand why I'm feeling so emotional. I've never given much thought before to how important it is to shed blood. I remember the feeling I had when Adam and Eve sinned. I think about God's plan. I can hear Jesus in my head saying, 'I will be killed.' I don't want to think about it. I can't.

Uncle Jacob and his friend take the dead lamb over to some hooks on the walls. They hang it on one of the hooks and start skinning it. I watch them, but I'm fighting with myself to stop thinking about what all of this means. The Passover, the sacrificed lamb, the blood on the altar, God's plan, Jesus being killed. It all seems to tie together somehow. I just have to stop thinking so hard.

They finish with the lamb and we head across the courtyard. Celebrating Passover is such an important thing to all the Jewish people. The Temple Mount is filled with people coming to offer their sacrifices.

It doesn't take long to get home with our portion of the lamb for our Passover meal. Aunt Sarah is busy getting the house clean. We all step up to help. Grandpa cleans the table. Dad cleans the stove. I help Uncle Jacob wash and dry all the wine goblets and plates that are used once a year for this very special occasion. Aunt Sarah starts setting the table with the dishes and wine goblets.

We all stand back and wait for Aunt Sarah to tell us what else to do. "Go!" she says. "There isn't anything more to do except fix the food for our meal. And I don't really need your help with that."

We all look at each other like, *Where are we going to go?*

Aunt Sarah looks at us, smiling. "Jacob, how about you take them to the synagogue? You can say some prayers."

Uncle Jacob gives his hands a clap. "I guess we're going to the synagogue. Who wants to go?"

I don't hesitate to answer. "Yes! We haven't been there yet."

Dad raises his hand, saying, "I'm in."

Grandpa stands up. "Me too!"

"Well, come on," Uncle Jacob says and leads the way out the door. "It's just a couple blocks from here."

I remember seeing a lot of synagogues yesterday, but we didn't stop at any of them. I'm curious.

"Uncle Jacob, how many synagogues are there in Jerusalem?"

"Oh, I'm not sure, but every community has one. Most of them are small. You'll find a couple of big synagogues over on the west side of town. They're for the rich people."

Before he finishes talking, we're there. We walk in and sit down on one of the benches. There are chairs up front on a platform. That's in case a chief priest or leader happens to show up. Uncle Jacob points to a man and says, "He's the head of our synagogue."

This place doesn't seem too different from our synagogue at home. I think they're all basically the same, except some read through the Torah in one year while others take three years to read through it. Anybody can ask to read or teach. If somebody disagrees with the teachings, the head of the synagogue settles any disagreements.

I can picture Jesus reading at the synagogue in Nazareth where he grew up. I wonder how many different synagogues he's been to. With a small thread of hope, I look around to see if he's here. He's not. Somewhere in the crowd, someone starts with a prayer. We all follow along like sheep that have taken this path a hundred times. Then we sing psalms. That's my favorite part.

We finish singing, and someone begins reciting, "Blessed are You, Lord our God. Hear, O Israel, the Lord our God, the Lord is one."

Then there's silence so we can say our own prayers. I pray for Jesus to be safe. I ask God to help me have faith in his plan.

The head of the synagogue steps up on the platform. He takes out a scroll and starts to read. It's Passover, so he's reading the story about Pharaoh and the plagues. I can't help but think about what I saw and experienced in Egypt. I'll never forget the sound of that whip. I'm glad God saved the Hebrews from that.

I smile, thinking about how much fun I had splashing along the walls of water at the Red Sea. It's quiet now and I realize I missed both the reading and the teaching. I wish Dad would believe me so I can tell him what I saw. My thoughts drift back to God's plan and Jesus dying. Passover, the sacrificed lamb, and Jesus dying has to all be tied together somehow.

Dad and Grandpa would know what to do to help Jesus. Uncle Jacob knows everything that goes on. Maybe he would know what to do. But then I shouldn't be hoping Jesus won't die. It's part of God's plan. And I have to trust God's plan. But it's hard.

The service ends with prayers. I listen to the conversations around me as we get up to leave.

"Do you think Jesus will celebrate Passover in Jerusalem?"

"I wouldn't, if I were him. Our leaders are out to destroy him."

"But he's the Savior God promised to send. Don't they see that?"

"I hope he becomes king of Judah and gets rid of the Romans."

With that, everyone starts talking, and it's almost too noisy to hear any one of them.

Uncle Jacob eyes the crowd, then motions for us to follow him. "I want you to meet my friend Zedekiah," he says. "He's the synagogue attendant." (That means he takes care of the building.)

Uncle Jacob told us the first day we got here about his friend named Zedekiah. I remember because he said Zedekiah knows everything that's going on in Jerusalem. Uncle Jacob makes the introductions. After a few minutes, Zedekiah pulls Uncle Jacob away from the crowd. I shuffle away with them.

Zedekiah whispers to Uncle Jacob, "The leaders are going to do something during Passover. I don't know what, but one of Jesus's disciples is helping them."

Uncle Jacob looks surprised.

I interrupt. "Yesterday, when we were at Caiaphas's palace—"

Uncle Jacob stops me. "Not so loud, Abe." He turns back to Zedekiah and whispers, "But he's right. Yesterday, we saw one of Jesus's disciples—I think it was Judas—leaving the council building. In fact, he was running like he didn't want anyone to see him."

My heart starts pounding. I can't help but be afraid for Jesus.

Uncle Jacob whispers again to Zedekiah. "Let me know if you hear anything. I don't care what hour it is. I want to know. Okay?"

Zedekiah nods and promises to tell. Then he turns to Grandpa and Dad and says, "Nice to meet you. Shalom." He disappears into the crowd before they can answer back.

Uncle Jacob introduces Dad and Grandpa to other people, but I'm not paying attention. I can't, because all I can think about is Jesus and the trouble he's in. I'm sure that between Dad, Grandpa, and Uncle Jacob, one of them would know what to do to help Jesus.

But if this is God's plan, then they shouldn't do anything. I'm so confused.

I sit down on a bench below the crowd and tune out all the noise. I clasp my hands together, close my eyes, and pray. "God, help me to have faith in your plan. Help me to trust you. Help me to not be scared. But most of all, please help Jesus."

We're in the synagogue for a long time. I don't mind, because it gives me time to say my prayers over and over.

Some time later, Dad nudges my shoulder. "Time to go, Abe," he says.

When we get outside, I look at the sun. Uncle Jacob does too. We can tell it's after lunchtime by where the sun is.

"We have plenty of time," Uncle Jacob says. "What do you say we just take a short, quiet walk? It will help clear our heads before we celebrate Passover."

"That's a great idea," Grandpa says.

Dad and Uncle Jacob lead the way, and Grandpa and I follow behind them. I guess "quiet walk" means no talking, because nobody is saying a word. I'm fine with that, because I have too much to think about.

Zedekiah said the leaders are going to do something to Jesus during Passover. And one of his disciples is helping them. But what can they do? If anything happens, Zedekiah will let us know. I pray again, "Please help Jesus. Please help me to have faith in your plan." Over and over I pray.

I don't pay any attention to where we are or how long we've been walking. Finally, Uncle Jacob breaks the silence. "We're almost home. It'll be time to start the Passover celebration soon."

The sun has gotten much lower in the sky. The walk was good because I spent most of it praying. I know God has a plan. But no matter how much I pray, deep down I don't want anything bad to happen to Jesus. I don't think that's bad of me. It just means I love him.

* * *

We get home, and Aunt Sarah has everything ready. Jeremiah is sitting at the table with his hands in his lap. I'm sure Aunt Sarah has warned him not to touch anything. We wash up and change into clean clothes.

We take turns as Uncle Jacob washes our feet, then Dad washes Uncle Jacob's feet. We each ceremoniously wash our hands, then take our places at the table. It's set with dishes, lamps, wine, unleavened bread, vegetables, bitter herbs, a bowl of vinegar, and charoset.

The charoset is a sticky, sweet food. It's supposed to remind us of the mortar the Hebrews used to make bricks when they were slaves. I rub my arm and remember what it felt like to be covered with that mud.

Grandpa is at the head of the table. He prays, "Blessed are you, O Lord our God, who has created the fruit of the vine. Blessed are you, O Lord our God. You have kept us alive, sustained us, and enabled us to enjoy this season."

Grandpa fills his goblet with wine. He takes a sip, then passes it to Uncle Jacob, who is sitting next to him.

Grandpa recites, "I am the Lord, and I will bring you out from under the yoke of the Egyptians."

Next, Grandpa passes the bitter herbs and vinegar. I think about that old man who was whipped and kicked because he fell. It was really bitter for him. But all the Hebrews were part of God's plan. I wonder if they knew that. I wonder if they would have been willing to be slaves if they had a choice.

Jeremiah is too young, so it falls on me to ask the traditional questions. "Why is this night different?" The questions and Grandpa's answers are all part of the Passover celebration.

I'm not listening very closely like I should. I'm thinking about Abraham and how he moved west when God asked him to.

I'm proud that God chose the Jewish people to save the world through. They haven't always been perfect in doing what God wants them to do. They struggled with their faith, but their faith survived.

I realize Grandpa has finished answering my question. Quickly I ask, "Why do we eat unleavened bread, bitter herbs, and roasted meat?"

I think back to Isaiah. I can still see him in that gathering. I remember the tears running down his cheeks when he shared the vision he'd had of Jesus. And now, Jesus is here, and I've seen him!

I wonder where Jesus is having his Passover meal. I wonder if it's in that building where we saw his disciples yesterday. I finish reciting the questions, but it's hard to listen to Grandpa's answers with all these thoughts in my head.

Aunt Sarah brings the roasted lamb to the table. I think this is the first Passover that I feel so proud to be Jewish. It just seems so real to me this year. I'm glad I got to see Jesus, to hear him teach, and to see him do miracles. I'll never forget any of it.

The platter of lamb is passed to me, and it makes me remember what Isaiah said about Jesus being like a lamb, taken to the slaughter. *Is Jesus our sacrifice?* I almost gasp out loud. I look around to see if anyone saw my reaction, but no one did.

The celebration goes on with eating, drinking, and the prayers. But I can't stop thinking about Jesus being a sacrifice, like a lamb. I love the Passover celebration. But this year I've been so caught up in thinking about everything I've seen and thinking about Jesus, I kind of missed the whole Passover celebration! I listen to Grandpa pray the last prayer.

It's late when we finish. I help clear the table, then I join the men by the fire. Nobody's talking. Finally, I ask, "Dad, may I be excused to go to bed?"

"Of course," he says. "Sleep well."

Jeremiah is already in bed, so I try to be quiet when I go upstairs. I change into my bedclothes and crawl under the blanket. I don't think I'll sleep for a while. Too many things are going on in my head. I get up on my knees in the bed and lean out the window. I'm sure Zag can see me. I think about all the things I saw on my adventure, and I smile.

I do feel sad when I think about how some of my ancestors let God down. But then a lot of the Hebrew people were faithful and loved God. Like Noah, Samuel, Daniel, David, and all those kings who were good leaders. And the prophets who spent their lives reminding people that God loves them. Hmm. Looking back, it's obvious why God chose my people to be part of his plan.

My bed moves, and I jump. Oh! It's Zag!

I start to talk, but Zag puts his hand to my mouth with a quick "*Shhh*."

"They won't believe me that I went on that adventure with you," I whisper.

"I know," he says, "but I promise, one day they will."

We grin at each other in the dark, and then he says, "I just wanted to make a quick stop. Things have already started to happen. I wanted to remind you to have faith in God's plan."

I can't help it, but my voice squeaks as I ask, "What do you mean, things have started to happen?"

Zag motions for me to be quiet. "I only have a minute, and this is important. You know how some of God's chosen people were really great and some were really bad?"

How does he always know what I'm thinking? I nod my head and say, "Yeah."

"Okay, so I want you to think of God's plan this way. Remember that tapestry you saw in the market yesterday that was only half done?"

I know better than to ask how he knows that. I just say, "Yeah."

"Well, God's plan to save the world is like that tapestry. God's plan—the tapestry—started with creation. Every situation and every decision that has ever been made, good or bad, is like another stitch with a different color in that tapestry. Being slaves in Egypt, the battles won and lost, the Babylonians, and even the Romans—they're all part of it."

Zag looks me straight in the eye. "Even the high priest Caiaphas, the Sadducees, and the Pharisees are part of the tapestry. Things will get bad over the next few hours. But you must be brave and remember the tapestry isn't finished yet. When it is, it will be beautiful. Just have faith in God's plan."

I want to say something, but Zag is gone.

Suddenly, I hear someone knocking on the door downstairs. It's late, and people should be home sleeping, I think. Then I remember that Zag said things were already happening. Is something happening to Jesus? Is someone at the door to tell us that news?

I get dressed as fast as I can and race downstairs. There's only the light from the fireplace, but I can see Uncle Jacob at the door talking to Zedekiah.

"Oh no," I cry. "What's wrong?"

CHAPTER 11

DAY 1—GUILTY

Dad and Grandpa come out of their bedroom.

"Is everything all right?" Dad asks.

Uncle Jacob pulls Zedekiah inside and closes the door. Quietly, he says, "Zedekiah came to tell us they've arrested Jesus."

Zag was right. Whatever is going to happen has begun. But what is it?

"Arrested!" Dad exclaims. "For what?"

"The disciple named Judas betrayed him. I don't know what he said or why they arrested Jesus. All I know is they took him to Annas, the priest. Of course, Annas can't make any decisions, so they'll probably take Jesus to Caiaphas."

We're all speechless. We can't believe what we're hearing.

"Dad, can we go to Caiaphas's palace? I want to see what they're going to do to Jesus. It's not that far from here. Can we?"

Dad and Uncle Jacob look at each other like, *should we?*

Grandpa clears his throat. "Normally I would say we should stay home at this hour of night." He stops talking and scratches his head.

I can't wait. I have to ask, "What do you think, Grandpa?"

Grandpa holds up his hand because he's still thinking. Then he says, "We all believe Jesus is the Savior God promised to send, right?"

We all agree.

"We also know there isn't anything Jesus did to give them reason to arrest him." He pauses again and rubs his chin. "What we don't know is what Judas said or did to make that happen."

Grandpa goes on, and he almost sounds afraid. "If they were able to convince one of his disciples to betray Jesus, it seems like our leaders are willing to do almost anything to make Jesus go away."

"I don't think there's anything we can do to change what's happening," Uncle Jacob says. "But I do want to know what's going on."

"Me too," Dad says.

I know it's not my decision, but in my heart, I'm saying "me too!"

Grandpa says quietly, "I agree. We have a chance to witness something here. I'm not sure if it's going to be good or bad. But I have a feeling this will be something people will remember for thousands of generations. And I think Abe should go."

I look at Dad and wait for him to agree. I can't breathe. My head is screaming *please let me go*, but the words don't come out.

Dad looks at me for a long minute. Then he says, "I tell you you're too young for a lot of things, Abe. It's why we didn't let you go on our last trip. And that was a mistake. But I know your heart, and I've seen your love for Jesus. Yes, I agree with Grandpa. You can go with us."

I grab my dad and hug him as hard as I can. My voice is muffled against his chest as I exclaim, "Thank you, Dad!"

Aunt Sarah comes out to see what all the commotion is about. She's surprised to see Zedekiah. Uncle Jacob tells her what's happening, and it makes her nervous.

Zedekiah says, "I'm not going to go with you. Just let me know what you find out."

Uncle Jacob opens the door for him. "Okay," he says. "I will as soon as I can. Shalom." Then he shuts the door behind Zedekiah and says, "The evening air feels a little chilly. We'd better put on a second layer of clothes."

We all go back to our rooms for more clothes. I'm the first one back, waiting at the door. I think I'm more scared than anything. I don't know what to expect.

We step out into the night. The moon is so bright, it makes it easy to see where we're going. Uncle Jacob takes a shortcut that gets us to the palace in half the time it took yesterday. The entrance is open, and the courtyard is full of people.

The council building is all lit up. Something is definitely going on. Fires are burning in all three fire pits. People huddle around them, trying to stay warm. We make our way over to the left side of the courtyard and push our way into the crowd. They're arguing about what happened when Jesus was arrested. We want to hear what they're saying.

"Hey, look," one says. "I'm telling you, I was there when they arrested Jesus. I saw the leaders and officers following that Judas disciple off the Temple Mount. I knew something was going on, so I followed them."

The arguing stops, and everyone listens.

"They knew Jesus was somewhere on the Mount of Olives. That disciple led them right to him. He was praying in the garden of Gethsemane."

"Did he put up a fight?"

"No. It was like he wasn't surprised to see them at all. They arrested Jesus with no problem, but one of the other disciples, Peter, had a sword. He swung it at the high priest's servant and cut off his ear!"

Everyone gasps.

"Yeah, but then Jesus told him to put the sword down! He said his Father could send twelve legions of angels if he asked him to. Then he said, 'Shouldn't I drink the cup my Father has given me to drink?' I don't know what that meant, but the disciples did. They backed off."

The crowd starts to talk, but the man continues. "But wait! That's not the crazy part. So Jesus picks up the ear. He cups his hand over the side of that guy's head and he heals him!"

"Wait," someone says. "Jesus put his ear back on?"

The man holds up his hand like he's making an oath. "I swear, I saw it with my own eyes. I know it's hard to believe." Shaking his head, he mutters, "I almost can't believe it myself."

The crowd starts asking questions. "Did they arrest any of the disciples?"

"No. After they tied Jesus up, his followers all ran off. We followed them to the priest Annas's house. I don't know what Annas said or did. We waited outside until they came out. Then we followed them here. That's all I know."

I don't understand how one of Jesus's own disciples could betray him. He must have gotten paid a lot of money to do that.

"It's strange, isn't it," Dad says quietly, "that Jesus wasn't surprised to see them?"

Dad doesn't know what Jesus knows—that he has to die to save us. Just then I realize that Jesus knows he can ask his Father to send angels to save him.

The thought of that shocks me. I realize this isn't a done deal. Jesus can change his mind if he wants to! I wonder what Zag would do if Jesus asked the angels to rescue him. But I know he won't. Jesus will drink that cup his Father gave him to drink.

Two officers come out of the hall. They walk through the crowd hollering, "Is there anyone who can testify against Jesus? The Sanhedrin wants to hear what you have to say. Is there anyone?"

A lot of people raise their hands. What can they possibly say against Jesus? The officers take them inside the hall and shut the doors.

We stand there for a long time but don't hear anything new.

Grandpa says, "Let's walk over to the other side of the courtyard. Maybe we'll hear something over there."

We push our way through the people to the other side. Grandpa was right. We start listening.

"I was in the hall, and I heard them. The Sanhedrin is determined to find Jesus guilty of something. People are accusing him of all kinds of stuff. Unfortunately for them, they can't get two people to agree to anything."

"Is Jesus okay?"

"They have him tied up. He's standing in front of the Sanhedrin listening to everything. The room is packed. I was forced to leave when they brought in more witnesses."

"Is Jesus saying anything to defend himself?" Uncle Jacob asks.

"Caiaphas asked him what he's been teaching. Jesus said he's taught openly in the synagogues and the temple. Jesus tells him to go ask the people what he taught." The man shakes his head and says, "They didn't like that answer. One of the officers slapped Jesus right across the face."

The crowd has a mixed reaction to that.

"Anyway, I guess they decided to take his advice. They sent officers outside. They had orders to bring in anyone who would testify against Jesus. I can't believe some of the stuff people are saying in there. But the leaders obviously want to hear it. They're looking for anything that will condemn him."

"But what are they accusing him of?"

"Stupid stuff, but none of it can be confirmed by a second person. That means they can't use it against Jesus."

Grandpa motions toward the fire nearest the hall doors. "Looks like there's room by that fire. I'm starting to feel cold. Let's go over there and warm up a little."

We make our way over, and the fire does feel good. I've been so caught up with what everyone is saying that I haven't realized just how cold I am. The doors open, and everybody looks up to see what's happening. They let one of the witnesses out, and then they leave the doors open. Two officers step out to be sure nobody goes in.

I can see Jesus inside. His hands are tied together with a rope, and he's just standing there with his head down. I feel so bad for him, but what can any of us do? Those leaders have no idea what is happening here. If they only knew who Jesus really is, if they would just take the time to get to know how kind and gentle he is, they would see how much love Jesus has for all the people, including them.

If they only knew this was the promised Messiah, they wouldn't treat him this way, I know it. There's a huge lump in my throat. I swallow hard.

Grandpa pokes me and points to the right side of the hall. "Look, Abe. That's the council of the Sanhedrin. It includes chief priests, Pharisees, Sadducees, and leaders. Some of Jerusalem's wealthiest citizens are there. The man sitting in the middle is Caiaphas, the high priest."

I look at Caiaphas, and I'm filled with anger. But then I hear Zag saying, *Caiaphas is part of the tapestry.* I try hard not to be angry.

Grandpa points at the people behind Jesus and says, "See those people? They aren't just there to watch. A lot of them are there to testify against Jesus."

The anger builds up inside of me again. I pray, "God, help me to trust you." I forget about my anger when I notice two men at the door. The officer lets one of them in, but the other one just stands at the door and watches. He looks familiar.

A lady from inside walks over and looks at him. "You were with Jesus," she says.

The man drops his head and says, "No, I don't know him." He runs down the steps and comes over to our fire.

We don't say anything to him, but I recognize him. It's the disciple Peter. Why would he say he doesn't know Jesus? He must be really scared to say that.

We all stand there watching, trying to hear what's happening inside. It seems like the same thing over and over. Someone testifies against Jesus, the Sanhedrin listen, and the people in the room demand justice. But then no one will confirm that charge, and they dismiss the witness and bring up another one.

We stay by that fire and watch the witnesses come and go for hours. Finally, it looks like the Sanhedrin doesn't have any more people to testify against Jesus. I'm glad, because that means they'll have to let Jesus go.

But then someone steps forward and hollers, "I heard Jesus say he can destroy the temple. He even said he can build another one in three days."

Another person stands up and shouts, "Yeah! I heard him say that too."

"Is that true?" Caiaphas asks Jesus. "You said that?"

Jesus just stands there with his head down, saying nothing.

"They can't condemn him for saying that," Grandpa says. "I don't care how many witnesses they have."

Caiaphas stands up. He looks tired and frustrated. He throws his hands up in the air and yells at Jesus, "I'm begging you. By the living God, just tell us if you are the Messiah. Are you the Son of God?"

Jesus calmly lifts his head and says, "One day, you will see the Son of Man sitting at the right hand of God." The crowd starts to holler, and I can't hear what Jesus says next.

Caiaphas puts his hands on his ears and screams, "Blasphemy! Blasphemy!"

He steps down from the platform, and grabbing his robe with both hands, rips it open. He screams again, "Blasphemy!" Then he walks over to Jesus and pokes him in the chest, screaming over and over, "Blasphemy! Blasphemy!"

He turns to the Sanhedrin. "We don't need to hear any more witnesses. Everyone has heard his blasphemy." He points to the Sanhedrin and yells, "What do you say?"

It's like they've been waiting for this very moment all night. They all stand up, and one by one, they condemn Jesus. "Guilty! Worthy of death."

CHAPTER 12

DAY 1—NO JUSTICE

With the verdict in place, the officers start to beat him. One of them puts a rag over Jesus's head and demands, "Prophesy! Tell us who hit you!" They hit him again and again. We stare into the hall, not believing what we're seeing. The spectators in the hall even turn against Jesus and begin spitting at him.

Jesus is on his knees now with his head down. We're all in shock at what's happening. We can only stand there and watch. People are leaving the council building, and two of them walk down to our fire. One of them takes a second look at Peter and says, "Hey! Aren't you one of his disciples?"

Peter keeps his head down. "No, I'm not."

The other one looks more closely at him. "Yes, you are," he says. "You're the one with the sword. You cut off my cousin's ear when they arrested Jesus!"

Peter looks up and says, "I don't know what you're talking about, man. I don't know him."

I can tell they don't believe him, but they stop asking.

Just then, I hear a rooster crowing in the distance. The sun should be coming up soon. It's still dark out, but the hall is so lit up, I can see Jesus clearly. He turns his head and looks out the door. I'm sure he's looking right at Peter. I look at Peter, and he sees Jesus looking at him too.

A sob breaks out of Peter's mouth as he throws his arm up to hide his face. Then he pushes his way through the crowd and disappears.

Everyone is abandoning Jesus! He must feel awful. Why are they all turning against him? All he ever did was heal people and make their lives better.

The lump starts to grow in my throat again. I swallow hard and fight back the tears.

Caiaphas walks over to the Sanhedrin, and he looks troubled. "By our own law, we cannot recognize this trial because it was conducted in the middle of the night," he says. "We'll have to meet back here as soon as the sun comes up. We'll charge him again just to be safe."

They all agree.

Caiaphas turns to the officers. "Take Jesus to a cell. As soon as you see the sun coming up, bring him back."

It seems to be over. The crowd outside begins to walk away.

Grandpa shakes his head back and forth in dismay. "Wow. Just when I thought they were going to have to let Jesus go, everything changed." He looks up at the eastern sky and says, "We might as well stay. The sun will be up soon. I want to be here when they do their *official* trial." There's no mistaking the sarcasm in his voice.

I don't want to go home. Too much is happening.

Uncle Jacob is upset. "How in the world are they going to justify killing Jesus? By what Jewish law can they do that?"

Grandpa shakes his head again. "I don't know, Jacob. I don't think they can kill Jesus."

I know what Zag told me, but Grandpa's words give me a little hope.

* * *

The sun rises, and the Sanhedrin members all come back and take their seats. Caiaphas comes in last and takes his seat in the center. As soon as he sits, the officers bring Jesus back in. They make him stand in front of the Sanhedrin, right where he was before.

We watch and listen as the Sanhedrin asks Jesus again, "Are you the Christ?"

"If I tell you," Jesus answers, "you still won't believe me."

"Are you the Son of God?"

"You say that I am."

And that's it. They don't want to hear any more. The formal trial is over. They condemn Jesus to death . . . again. Caiaphas tells the chief priests to take Jesus to Pilate.

Grandpa throws up his hands and spins around. "Ah, so that's how they're going to do it. They condemn Jesus to death, but they're going to let the Romans carry out the sentence."

"Grandpa, no! That means the soldiers will crucify Jesus on that hill. Right?"

Grandpa answers slowly. "Well, that's their way. But I'm not so sure Pilate will agree to it. Jesus hasn't broken any Roman laws."

That gives me a small bit of hope to hang onto. It allows me to breathe again. Yet deep down inside, I know Jesus will still have to die.

The chief priests and leaders leave the hall. By now Jesus looks weak and tired. The officers have to take Jesus by his arms so he can keep up with them.

"They're heading to Herod's palace where Pilate is staying," Uncle Jacob says.

Grandpa takes off behind them. "Come on, men. Let's follow them and see what happens."

I think I have the best grandpa ever. There isn't anything I would rather be doing than finding out what's happening to Jesus. We take the same route we did the other day, except now the market is quiet. We walk up the steps and take the tiled walkway around the fountain to the center building.

They lead Jesus into the hall and let us follow them in. Pilate isn't there yet, but we don't have to wait very long for him. Two big doors spring open at the back of the hall, and there he sits. Pilate is up on a platform, sitting in a fancy chair with soldiers on both sides.

It's a courtroom, and Pilate is the only judge. He will decide the fate of Jesus. He motions for the chief priests and officers to come forward into the courtroom. They go in, and the officers follow with Jesus. They put him right in front of Pilate and back away, leaving Jesus standing there alone.

We move in as close as the soldiers will let us. We don't want to miss a word.

"What's this about?" Pilate asks.

"This man is perverting our nation," one of the leaders calls out.

Pilate holds his hands out like, *so what?*

"He forbids us to pay taxes to Caesar."

"But yet they do." Pilate looks bored.

Someone else hollers, "He says he's the Messiah, a king."

Pilate seems to find that interesting. He looks at Jesus and asks, "Are you the king of the Jews?"

Without looking up, Jesus answers, "You say so."

Pilate smiles at Jesus. Then he looks at the leaders and says, "I find no basis to accuse this man." He stands up to walk away.

"I didn't think he'd condemn Jesus," Grandpa says. He sounds relieved.

But the leaders are frantic to convince Pilate to condemn Jesus. They all start shouting at the same time.

"He stirs up the people with his teaching!"

"He's got the people in Jerusalem all stirred up!"

"Yeah, and not just Jerusalem, either—it's all over Judea and Galilee."

Pilate stops, turns back to them, and asks, "Is Jesus from Galilee?"

"Yes."

"Well, that's Herod's area. This is his problem, not mine. Herod is in town for the Passover. Take Jesus to him." He pulls his robe around himself, turns, and walks out.

The chief priests and leaders turn to leave the hall. They motion for the officers to get Jesus.

"Let's go," Grandpa says. "They're going to the Hasmonean palace."

The crowd is growing, but we manage to stay together. We walk the same route we did two days ago. When we make the right turn, I look over at that hill. It sends chills up my back. I don't want to even think about Jesus ending up on that hill. He just can't.

I whisper under my breath, "Please, God, not that hill."

We get to the Hasmonean palace, and the courtyard fills up with the crowd really fast. Everyone is watching the balcony, waiting for Herod Antipas.

But I'm looking at Jesus. He seems so tired and worn out. He just stands there with his head down, so quiet and humble.

I wonder if Jesus saw that hill when we walked past it. I wish I could do something so he knows he's not alone. I feel the crowd squeezing and pushing us toward the front. I almost fall when the officers push us back to make room for the leaders.

Finally, Herod Antipas comes out on the balcony with ten other people. He's not what I expected at all. He's fat like that statue of King Herod. His robe has gold woven into it that matches the gold chains around his neck. His dark beard is trimmed short, and a golden crown holds down his dark, long, curly hair.

He seems delighted to see Jesus. He looks at Jesus and says, "At last, I get to meet the healer. You are the man of miracles. Tell me, how do you do it? Is it magic? Can you see the future?" He turns to the people behind him and laughs at his own stupid humor.

They laugh with him, but I can tell they're afraid of him.

He looks back at Jesus, still laughing. "Please, do a miracle for me. Do just a small one." He waits, but Jesus just stands there, not saying a word. Herod Antipas stops laughing and anger fills his round face. The leaders use that moment to take turns accusing Jesus.

"He's leading our nation astray."

"He says he's the Messiah."

"He claims to be the king of Judah."

Herod doesn't pay much attention until they say "king of Judah." Then he turns and stares at the leader who said it. That person gets so scared that he backs up to disappear into the crowd.

Herod looks back at Jesus and says, "Oh, so you're a king now? You don't look like a king." He points to his soldiers and orders, "Give the king a robe that's fit for a king."

I don't know where the robe comes from, but they throw a fancy robe over Jesus's shoulders, covering the red robe he's wearing.

The soldiers surround Jesus and push him back and forth among each other, laughing. One of them gives Jesus a push and says, "Your king!" Another soldier catches Jesus and gives him another push saying, "No, *your* king." They push him back and forth. Herod laughs at the game his soldiers are playing. The fancy robe falls to the ground.

Then Herod puts both hands on his fat belly and says, "That was fun. Now take him back to Pilate. This is his problem." Herod disappears off the balcony. The soldiers grab the robe on the ground and go back into the palace.

"I think they're getting worried." Uncle Jacob is watching the leaders. "Herod isn't going to do their dirty work either."

"They're going to have to convince Pilate." Grandpa looks around and says, "The crowd is growing." Grandpa sounds uneasy. "Be ready to follow the leaders as soon as they start to leave."

Grandpa was right. The religious leaders motion for the officers to get Jesus, then head back to see Pilate. We follow right behind them, but the crowd keeps growing. I'm not surprised that so many people have come out this early to see what's happening. Jesus helped a lot of people.

We stay as close as we can behind them all the way back to Pilate's palace. We're close enough to get into the hall before it fills up. We don't wait very long before the doors open again. I see Pilate in his fancy chair with his soldiers standing beside him. This time, a woman is standing next to him. She must be his wife, because she's resting her arm on his shoulder.

The leaders move up close to Pilate with Jesus. Pilate's irritated voice rings through the room. "What is this? I told you before—I do not find this man guilty of any charges."

"Thank you, God," I whisper.

Pilate taps his fingers on the arm of his chair as he thinks. He gets a crafty smile on his face. "The previous governor had a custom for Passover. He would release a prisoner during this time of year. I'll do the same thing. I'll have Jesus flogged, then I'll release him." Pilate seems happy with his solution. He doesn't want to crucify Jesus.

The leaders huddle to talk, then one hollers out, "Release Barabbas instead."

I catch my breath. I don't know who Barabbas is, but Pilate wouldn't do that, would he?

Pilate is surprised too. "But Barabbas is a murderer," he protests. "You want me to release a murderer? What am I supposed to do with Jesus?"

The leaders begin to yell.

"Crucify him!"

"Crucify him!"

Even the crowd starts to chant, "Crucify him! Crucify him!"

Pilate says something to a soldier, who then runs out of the room. I watch the crowd chanting *crucify him* and I can't believe it. Jesus has done nothing but help them. And aren't these the same people who threw their coats and branches in front of him last week?

Jesus just stands there with his head down, waiting.

The crowd stops chanting when four soldiers come into the room with a man. He's dirty and has chains on his hands and feet.

Uncle Jacob mutters, "That's Barabbas."

Pilate holds his arms out and says, "What evil has this man Jesus done? I find nothing that deserves a death sentence. Even Herod Antipas didn't find him guilty."

But the crowd starts to chant again, "Crucify him! Crucify him!"

I hold my hands over my ears to block out their chants, but I still hear them.

Pilate stands up and walks over to a wash basin. That quiets the crowd for a moment. He washes his hands and dries them with a towel. He throws down the towel like he's angry. He turns and says, "I am innocent of the blood of this man."

He waves dismissively at the crowd. His disgust with them is clear as he leaves the room. The soldiers take Jesus from the officers and disappear through a doorway at the side of the room.

CHAPTER 13

DAY 1—THE LONG WALK

"Get out of our way!" One of the leaders shoves Uncle Jacob out of his way as the group pushes through the crowd.

"Let them through, Jacob," Grandpa says. "They have to go tell Caiaphas what's happening." The crowd follows, spilling into the street. We were right up front watching Pilate do his best to release Jesus, so we're some of the last to leave.

Grandpa leads us to the bench where we rested two days ago. "Let's just sit a moment and let this all settle in our heads." He sounds tired and sad.

We sit down, and I feel sick to my stomach. The worst that could happen is happening.

Suddenly, there's a loud commotion to our right. It's the soldiers from the hall, and they have Jesus. They're pushing him around and laughing.

"Oh, great and mighty king," a soldier taunts, "where are your followers now?"

"We're allowed to go back there," Uncle Jacob says. "Do we want to?"

Grandpa gets up. "Yeah. I think we should see this through to the end."

Dad puts his hand on my shoulder. "I think Abe and I will return to the house. You two go ahead."

"Dad, no! I want to go. I have to see Jesus. I want to be where he is!"

Dad looks back and forth from me to the soldiers. "You really do love him, don't you, son?" He looks unsure, but finally he says, "Okay. I don't know how long we'll stay, but we'll go."

The soldiers yank on Jesus's robe, pulling it and his undergarment off, leaving him nearly naked. They tie him to a tall post, and then two soldiers pick up whips. I remember the whips the soldiers used in Egypt . . .

These are so much worse. Six long leather straps are connected with a handle. Each strap has a sharp piece of metal on the end. I think I'm going to be sick.

Dad puts his arm around my shoulders and pulls me close.

"God," I pray, "don't let it hurt. Please don't let it hurt."

The soldier wields his whip. It cracks loudly in the air, and then it hits Jesus with a thud. Jesus cries out, and his body bounces against the pole. Blood pours out of the cuts on his back that the whip has made.

The soldier pulls back his whip just as the other soldier's whip hits Jesus. Again his body bounces, and blood runs from the cuts made on his shoulder. They take turns whipping Jesus over and over. His back, legs, and arms are all cut up. Dad's grip around me gets tighter with every crack of the whip. I want to hide my face, but I can't.

This is the price Jesus has to pay? This is the price to set us free from sin? My sin? Why does it have to be so horrible? I won't take my eyes off Jesus. I want him to know I'm here. I want him to know I love him.

They keep whipping him, and it feels like it's never going to stop, but then Jesus's whole body goes limp. The soldiers stride over to him, walking all over the ground that's soaked with his blood. They untie him and force him to stand.

I don't feel that knot in my stomach. I don't feel that lump in my throat. I just feel numb.

A soldier pulls some branches full of long thorns off a dead bush. He twists the branches together and bends them into a circle. He walks over to Jesus, a sneer on his face.

"So you're a king, huh?" He pushes the thorns down hard onto Jesus's head. "Here's your crown, king."

Jesus squints from the pain. Blood drips from where the thorns have torn through his skin.

"Wait!" Another soldier throws a purple robe over Jesus's shoulders. "A king needs a robe."

Jesus almost falls from the pain of the robe rubbing against his cuts.

They're all laughing and making jokes. Two soldiers spit at Jesus and the others chant, "Hail, King of the Jews."

A new commotion draws attention away from Jesus for a moment. Several soldiers come out of the building, leading two prisoners. More soldiers come from behind the building, carrying three wood beams.

They drop them on the ground in front of the prisoners. One of them gives the prisoners a shove. He points at the ground and says, "Pick up a beam and follow us."

The two prisoners stare at Jesus as they pick up their beams. The soldiers push them through the courtyard and into the street.

Uncle Jacob says, "It's not hard to figure out where they're going."

I stare at the third beam on the ground. I'm sure that one is for Jesus. The knot in my stomach gets tighter.

Just then another soldier comes out, and he must be in charge. "Enough of the games!" he hollers. "Get him to the hill."

I realize I've taken my eyes off Jesus. I look back in time to see his pain when they pull off the purple robe.

They drop his own garment back over his head and pull it down over his body. It wants to stick to his bloody skin. They put his robe on him, the red one that used to look so soft. It partially hides his blood-stained garment.

"Pick up your beam, king," the soldiers taunt. One of them lifts the beam and throws it over Jesus's shoulders. Jesus stumbles under the weight. I can't imagine how much that must hurt on all those cuts.

"They expect him to carry that to the hill?" Uncle Jacob says almost too loudly. I can hear the anger in his voice.

Jesus takes a couple steps to follow the soldiers. One end of the beam drops to the ground, but he's still holding the other end that's sitting on his shoulder. He follows the soldiers into the courtyard, dragging the beam behind.

They wait for Jesus as the beam bounces down from step to step. We stay close behind and follow them into the street. The other soldiers and their prisoners are way out ahead of us. The street is lined with people. It's so noisy, it's hard to understand what anyone is saying. Some are yelling mean things at Jesus, and others are in shock, like we are.

There are soldiers in front of and behind Jesus. They keep pushing the crowds back, but we stay as close as we can behind them. I can tell Jesus is in a lot of pain. He's really struggling to carry that beam. And then he drops under the weight of it. A soldier pulls him up and puts that beam across his shoulders again.

Jesus takes only two steps before one end of the beam slides down and hits the ground. He's dragging it again. A woman steps out of the crowd. I recognize her right away. "Look! That's Mary, Jesus's mother."

"You're right, Abe," Grandpa says. "It is."

It's a precious moment—a moment I wish time could stop for, when everything would freeze and give the two of them a few last moments. I can see the pain in her face and in her eyes. I can see her heart break as she looks at what they've done to her son.

But the soldiers don't have the patience to stop, not even for a mother. They push Jesus to move on.

Jesus isn't moving fast enough for them. A soldier hollers for them to stop, then he pulls a man out of the crowd to carry the wood beam. The pause allows a woman to step out of the crowd and wipe Jesus's face with a cloth. The soldiers push her back and shove Jesus forward.

Even without the beam, it's hard for Jesus to walk, and he falls again. The soldiers don't care that he's in pain. They pull him to his feet and thrust him forward again.

We're coming up to the turn for the Hasmonean palace. This time we don't make that turn. Instead, we turn left toward a gate that will take us outside the wall and to that hill.

Just before we go out the gate, a group of women step into the street. Jesus sees them weeping and gives them a look of love and compassion. He says something to them, but it's so noisy, I can't hear what he said.

The soldiers don't like it and keep him moving through the gate. Jesus falls again, and the soldiers yank him to his feet.

I really don't think Jesus is going to make it up that hill. I hope he doesn't. I don't want him to be crucified. I pray again, "God, please help Jesus. Don't let them crucify him. If he has to die, let it be now." But we keep moving forward.

CHAPTER 14

DAY 1—THE GREAT SACRIFICE

The crowd is thinning out as we make our way up the hill. I guess they don't want to watch what is going to happen up there.

The top of the hill is crowded with soldiers. I wonder where the other prisoners are. Three poles are sticking up out of the ground. A soldier is on a ladder at the pole to the right. Then I see one of the other prisoners lying on the ground at the foot of that pole.

His hands are nailed to that beam he carried to the hill. The soldiers lift him up and attach the beam to the pole. He just dangles there until another soldier pushes his feet up to a slanted platform on the pole. Then he nails the man's feet to it.

The second man is on the ground at the other pole. I don't watch what they do to him. Instead, I look for Jesus. He's standing by the middle pole, and they've taken his robe and garment again.

A soldier tries to give him a drink. "Roman law orders us to give you this drink," he says. "It helps with the pain." But Jesus refuses to drink it. The soldier throws the drink on the ground. "Your choice," he grunts.

He pushes Jesus down, and he lands on his back on the ground. He's still wearing that crown of thorns. It cuts deeper into his head when he hits the ground. A soldier pulls Jesus off the ground enough to shove the beam under his shoulders.

They stretch his arms out on the beam. I know what they're going to do, and I force myself to watch. They pound nails right through his hands and into the beam.

I feel like I'm going to be sick. I can't be sick, though, because Dad would make me go home. I can't go home. I have to stay here. I can't abandon Jesus. He has to know there are people here who love him, who won't leave him.

I watch them pull Jesus up and attach his beam to the pole. My head is spinning. I can hardly think straight. Everything is blurring together.

The soldiers leave Jesus dangling there until one of them gets down off the ladder. Then he pushes Jesus's feet up on the slanted platform to nail them down.

This time, I can't watch. I turn my head and see the temple. I can picture Jesus standing in the courtyard. I look back at Jesus and want all of this to be a nightmare. I want to just wake up and find out none of this is real. But I won't wake up, because it is real.

Dad gets our attention when he says, "Look! Pilate just brought a sign to be nailed to the top of Jesus's pole."

A soldier climbs up to nail it to the pole.

Grandpa waits for the soldier to get out of the way. Then he says, "It's in three languages. One of them I can read. It says, 'This is the king of the Jews.' It isn't much comfort, but it's the truth."

A chief priest reads the sign and yells at Pilate angrily. "That's wrong! You must change it. It should say, '*He said* he was the king of the Jews.'"

"What I have written," Pilate says, "I have written." Then he turns his horse to go down the hill.

The chief priests and leaders are angry. They start taunting Jesus.

"He saved others," one yells, "but he can't save himself!"

"You say you can destroy the temple and build it in three days? Well, if you can do that, then you can save yourself!"

They laugh together at the taunts, urging each other on.

"If you are the king of Israel, come down from the cross. Then we'll all believe you."

"Hey, he trusted in God. Let God deliver him. That is, if God will even have him. He claimed he was the Son of God."

Uncle Jacob pushes one of his hands through the air in disgust. "They're only saying that stuff because of that sign. They have to discredit Jesus so the crowd won't hate them for having him crucified."

The man being crucified to the left of Jesus hears all the taunting. He taunts Jesus too and says, "If you are Christ, save yourself and us!"

But the man crucified on the right doesn't like the sarcasm. "Don't you fear God? We deserve what we're getting. He doesn't." He calls over to Jesus, "Lord, when you get to your kingdom, please remember me."

Jesus turns his head so he can see him. Then he says, "Today, you will join me in paradise."

I can't believe with all the pain Jesus feels, he still loves us. He even loves that criminal.

One of the soldiers picks up Jesus's bloody garment. He rips it into four pieces and hands a piece to each soldier with him. "Here, I'll share this with you guys." Then he holds up Jesus's robe. "There aren't any seams in this robe. What do you say we just roll the dice for it?"

They agree, and with a toss of the dice, one of the soldiers wins Jesus's robe.

The soldiers can't leave, but a lot of the leaders who were taunting Jesus do. It's quiet on the hill now. Mary is standing near Jesus—some other women and one disciple are with her.

Suddenly, Jesus says to his mother, "Woman, he is your son."

Then, to the disciple, he says, "This is your mother."

That's so kind of Jesus to make sure someone will look after his mother like a son.

I think maybe three hours have gone by. The four of us have hardly even spoken. Grandpa gathers us in. "We haven't slept all night," he says. "We haven't had anything to eat either. I'm guessing it's about lunchtime. Is everybody still okay?"

Uncle Jacob says, "I'm good."

Dad looks at me. "How about you, son? Do you want to stay, or do you want to go home?"

Without taking my eyes off Jesus, I answer, "I'm good."

Dad gives me a squeeze and says, "I'm good too."

Grandpa nods at Dad. "Then it's settled. We stay to the end."

The women are still weeping. I look up, and the sun is at its highest point. I look back at Jesus. He was so willing to give up his life for us. I don't know anyone else who would be willing to die for somebody. And the way he's dying is horrible.

All of a sudden, everything gets dark. It's like the sun just went black. It gets so dark that I'm terrified. Even the soldiers are panicking.

"Our gods are angry. That's why it's dark," one of them says.

Another one argues, "Maybe the God of the Jews is angry for what we did to Jesus."

I wonder if the dark is God's way of looking away from the pain Jesus is feeling. It's hard to understand everything that's happening.

We stand there in the dark without taking our eyes off Jesus. Another couple of hours go by, maybe more.

Suddenly, Jesus cries out. "My God, my God. Why have you forsaken me?"

I feel so horribly bad for Jesus. I want to cry or scream or something. Jesus doesn't deserve this, none of this. I start to feel angry. I hate what they did to Jesus. I hate that he has to hang there in all that pain. I hate that we can't help him.

I clench my fists and close my eyes. I can see Zag. I hear him saying over and over, "Have faith in God's plan."

I forget my anger when I hear Jesus say, "I thirst."

One of the soldiers soaks a sponge in the stuff they tried to give Jesus before. Then he puts the sponge on the end of a long stick and lifts it up to Jesus's mouth. It's hard to see if Jesus drinks any of it. The soldier doesn't hold it there very long before dropping it on the ground.

Suddenly, Jesus cries out. "Father, into your hands I commend my spirit!" Moments later, he whispers, "It is finished." Then his head drops, and he is still.

We stand there, staring up at Jesus with his head bent down. None of us move, not even an inch. We all know what just happened.

CHAPTER 15

DAY 1—IT'S OVER

The women realize Jesus has just died, and they start crying again. It's over. The pain, the suffering, the mocking, it's all over. What Jesus came to earth to do is finished. I have such a huge feeling of loss. I feel empty inside. I feel like the world has just lost its greatest treasure. But at the same time, I'm glad Jesus isn't suffering anymore.

Suddenly, the ground begins to shake, and I grab onto Dad. All four of us grab on to each other, and Grandpa shouts, "It's an earthquake!"

Most of the people around us run down the hill and into the city.

Grandpa says, "I think we should just stay right where we are."

Uncle Jacob points to the tombs on the hill across from us and says, "Look! The rocks in front of the tombs are rolling away." We all look, and our mouths drop open at what we're seeing. People who died and were buried in those tombs are walking out.

The soldiers see it too. They're as shocked and scared as we are. One of the soldiers points to Jesus and says, "There is no doubt in my mind, this man was the Son of God!"

I knew that all along, but now he knows it too.

The ground stops shaking, and we let go of each other. We stay, because as long as Jesus is still hanging there, we don't want to leave.

Another hour or so goes by. A centurion comes up the hill with three men pulling a small cart. I can see folded linens in the cart. The centurion tells the soldiers, "Pilate wants these men dead before sunset. Go break their legs."

"Why?" I can't help the outburst. I feel disgusted and horrified. "Haven't they done enough to them?"

Uncle Jacob puts his hand on my back. "They can't breathe air out unless they push up on their feet," he explains. "That's why they're going to break their legs. They'll suffocate to death."

I cringe as a soldier breaks the legs of the prisoner to the right. I don't watch the one on the left, but I hear him scream. They don't touch Jesus, because he's already dead. But to be sure, they push a spear up into his side.

"Take the body down," the centurion orders. "Give it to that man over there." He points to one of the men who came up with him.

Why would a stranger want Jesus's body? What would he do with it?

Uncle Jacob sees my panic and puts his arm over my shoulders. "I've seen that man with Jesus many times. He's from Jerusalem. He's an honest, wealthy man named Joseph. I'm not sure if he's a disciple or not, but he's good. And it looks like they've brought linens to wrap around Jesus's body. Besides, it takes a very special person to be willing to touch a dead body on this holy day."

We watch as two soldiers climb ladders. They tie a rope around Jesus to hold him up while they pull him free from the nails. Then they carefully lower his body to the ground. I guess they're being respectful, now that they believe he was God's Son.

Mary is there to catch him as they let him down. She falls under the weight of his body and sits there, holding him on the ground. Carefully, she takes the thorns off his head. She's weeping the whole time.

The man with the linens kneels down and explains to Mary, "I'm Joseph. I knew your son. I would like to put Jesus in my tomb. It's never been used."

She nods her head, and he waits for her to have as much time as she needs with Jesus. When she's ready, the two other men wrap Jesus's bruised and bloody body with the linens enough to transport him, and they lay him in the cart.

Then they pull the cart down the hill and over to the tombs. Mary, the disciple, and the other women follow them. They put his body into a tomb and roll a huge stone in front of it. Then they walk away and disappear into the city.

It's over. Jesus is dead.

"I think it's time to go home," Grandpa says with a deep sigh.

We walk down the hill and in through the gate to the city. We stop and look down the street that Jesus walked just hours ago. We can still see his blood on the ground. I don't want to walk there, and I think no one else does either, because we just stand still.

Grandpa shakes his head and says, "Let's go up through the Temple Mount."

We turn left and walk past the Hasmonean palace. We go up the steps and onto the Temple Mount. A crowd is standing in front of the temple. *Now what?*

"What's going on?" Uncle Jacob asks.

"During the earthquake, the thick, heavy curtain that guards the most holy place was torn in two."

Uncle Jacob looks worried. He turns to us. "That is not good. Not at all. Let's get out of here."

It's painful to walk through the courtyard. I'm glad to have all those memories of Jesus, but now he's gone, and those memories hurt. We go into the tunnel, down the steps, and out the gate. There aren't many people in the streets, and by now, it's getting late.

We get home, and I feel dirty. I have to wash up. I stand at the basin and scrub my face over and over. I rub my hands with a rag, but I still feel dirty. Nothing can wash away what I saw today.

Aunt Sarah calls us to dinner, but I don't feel hungry. Still, Dad insists that I eat a little, so I mostly just push my food around my plate. Grandpa, Uncle Jacob, and Dad are talking, but the words don't register in my head. I don't want to listen because that means reliving what happened.

I pick at my food and think about Zag. He said Isaiah and King David both said the Messiah would rise. I find that confusing. Then I remember the conversation Jesus had with his disciples. That the gentiles—the Romans—would mock him, whip him, spit on him, and kill him. I get it now!

Wow, Jesus really did know everything that was going to happen to him. And I remember that Jesus also said he'd rise on the third day.

What did he mean? I can't ask Dad, because Dad still thinks it was all a dream. I just have to wait and see what happens in three days.

And that's when I hear Dad say, "We probably should think about heading back home tomorrow."

Without even thinking, I protest. "But, Dad, I thought we were staying for the whole eight days of the feast?"

Dad shakes his head. "With everything that's happened, I think it's best if we just head back home."

Oh no! I need to stay, to find out what happens on the third day. I have to say something, but I can't. What can I tell him to convince him to stay?

I just blurt it out. "Dad, I really want to stay a couple more days."

Dad looks at me strangely. "What for?"

"I know you think my adventure was just a dream, but please . . . I know something is going to happen on the third day. I don't want to leave until it does."

"What's going to happen?"

I put my head down and answer quietly, "I don't know."

Dad shakes his head. I have to convince him before he makes a decision he won't change.

"Please, Dad. I don't *know* what's going to happen in three days. But I *do* know that everything that's happened to Jesus is part of God's plan." My eyes fill with tears. With a raspy voice, I plead, "We have to have faith in God's plan. And God isn't done yet."

I wipe my eyes with my sleeve and beg, "Please. If nothing happens in three days, I won't ever bring up my adventure again. Can we please stay for just a couple more days?"

Dad looks at Grandpa like he doesn't understand. "What do you think?"

Grandpa shakes his head and turns his attention to me. "First, I have to ask, how did you know that was Jesus's mother this morning? You know, the woman who stepped out of the crowd?" Then, before I can answer, he says, "No, I don't want to know. Not tonight, that is."

He takes a deep breath, thinks for a moment, and then says, "I think we should let Abe have this one. I think we should stay a couple more days and see what happens."

"Okay," Dad says. "We'll stay."

I should be happy, but nothing can make me happy right now. I'm so sad for Jesus. All I want is to be alone. And I'm definitely not hungry. "Can I please be excused to go to bed?" I ask.

Dad looks at the food on my plate, then he looks at me. His eyes are tired too. "Of course you can go to bed," he says. "Good night, son."

Aunt Sarah smiles at me, then reaches over and gives my arm a squeeze. "Jeremiah and I will try to be quiet when it's time for him to go to bed."

"Thanks, Aunt Sarah." I give her a quick hug and go upstairs to my room.

I change my clothes and climb into bed. I can't sleep, though, because in my head I keep seeing everything that's happened. I try to push it all back, but it won't stop. I feel that lump in my throat again. I roll over to lie on my stomach and pull the blanket up over my head.

This time I don't swallow that lump in my throat. Instead, I push my face into the bed as hard as I can and cry. I cry so hard if feels like I've pushed all the air out of my lungs. I lift my head enough to gasp for breath, then cry some more.

At some point sleep takes over, and all those horrible things are no longer in my head.

CHAPTER 16

DAY 2 — THE DAY AFTER

I sleep so hard and for so long that I wake up and don't know what day it is. It's dark out, and I don't know if that means it's morning or evening. I don't want to get up and face what happened. But I don't want to lie in bed and think about it either. Finally, I get up, change my clothes, and go downstairs.

The table is set, and I can smell food cooking. I guess it's evening. I still feel tired, and I can't quit yawning. I could probably go right back to sleep, but I feel more hungry than I do tired. I haven't eaten much of anything since the Passover meal.

The baby is in her cradle, awake and making noises. Jeremiah is on the floor with his blocks. Dad, Grandpa, and Uncle Jacob come in from outside and look all rested up.

Dad sees me and says, "Good morning! Or maybe I should say good night?" They all laugh.

Aunt Sarah starts putting food on the table.

"Hey, Abe. You'll like this one." Uncle Jacob grins at me. "Our friend Zedekiah stopped by earlier. He told us that the chief priests and Pharisees went to Pilate again."

"What for?"

His grin gets bigger. "They're hearing rumors that Jesus said he'll rise again after three days. Isn't that interesting? There's that three days you keep talking about."

He waits for me to say something, but I don't. I don't know what to say.

"So they asked Pilate to post guards at the tomb," Dad adds. "They think the disciples will take the body and claim Jesus has risen from the dead."

That wakes me up better than a bucket of cold water. "Really? Wow!"

"Wow is right," Dad says. "I'm beginning to wonder about this adventure you say you had."

I look at him hopefully, but before I can say anything more, Uncle Jacob says, "We'd better sit down and eat. The food is getting cold. Abe, you must be starving!"

My stomach growls right on cue. Everyone laughs as I answer, "Yes, I am."

Aunt Sarah calls, "Come, Jeremiah, and sit down."

Uncle Jacob helps Jeremiah up on the bench. Aunt Sarah has already dished up his food and cut his meat. He's learned not to touch it until someone prays.

We all swing our legs over the benches and sit down. We wait for Grandpa to pray. I'm so hungry everyone can hear my stomach growl. When the prayer is over, I reach for the bread. It's still unleavened bread, but it's good.

Uncle Jacob drops some meat on his plate. He hands the serving dish to me and says, "Abe, your aunt Sarah cooked extra food tonight. She knows we're all hungry. Don't be shy. I know you have to be hungry too."

It smells so good, and he's right—I am hungry. But I start with a normal portion and pass the food along.

Once we've all been served, Uncle Jacob says, "Zedekiah told me that Jesus's disciples are all still in Jerusalem. That is, except Judas. We found out that the chief priests paid him thirty pieces of silver to betray Jesus. He felt so guilty later that he threw the coins at them and went out and hung himself."

I don't say anything. All I can think is that Judas was a sad part of that tapestry.

Uncle Jacob chews a big piece of meat and swallows it. Then he says, "The disciples are staying in a room not too far from here. Word is, even though Jesus is dead, they don't think it's over. They plan to keep teaching what Jesus taught them."

I'm glad to hear the disciples feel that way.

"The chief priests and leaders won't be happy about that," he continues. "It'll be interesting to watch what happens. Zedekiah always knows what's going on, so as soon as he knows, we'll know."

Other than Uncle Jacob, we eat mostly in silence. I think everyone is just too hungry to talk. I scrape my plate and eat the last bite. I still feel a little hungry, so I take another small piece of meat and some more bread. Dad and Uncle Jacob take more too. Grandpa takes more bread and soaks up the juices on his plate with it.

Jeremiah is done. He wrinkles his face when Aunt Sarah wipes it. "Go ahead, Jeremiah. You're excused. You can go play."

He runs over to his blocks on the floor and starts stacking them.

We all finish eating—probably more than we should have. Dad rubs his belly and says, "Thank you so much for that wonderful meal, Sarah. You've been so kind to us."

"You're very welcome. You know you're welcome here any time." She starts cleaning off the table. I grab some dishes and help until the table is cleared.

She smiles. "Thank you for your help, Abe, but you can go sit by the fire now. I'm sure you want to hear everything they have to say."

"Yeah, I do. Thanks!" I join the men by the fire, and it feels good. It's not a big fire. Just enough to take the chill out of the night air that wants to seep in. The wood cracks and pops as the fire consumes it. Flames roll out in every direction. The smoke drifts up the chimney into the black night outside. Inside, we're all quiet, totally captivated by the flames. But all I can think about is what happened and what will happen next.

I'll never forget what I felt when Adam and Eve sinned. Everything changed. I felt it when the barrier went up between God and us.

I remember that swirling pillar of fire holding back Pharaoh and his army at the Red Sea. That was God's presence, protecting the Hebrews.

I think about how God's presence is in the temple behind that big, thick, heavy curtain. And how only the high priest gets to go into that most holy place.

Then it hits me—that big, thick, heavy curtain was torn in two during the earthquake. The earthquake that happened right after Jesus died! I sit up straight as if a bolt of lightning hit me. *It makes perfect sense!*

My reaction doesn't go unnoticed. "What's wrong, Abe?" Dad asks.

I start thinking out loud. "Jesus is the promised Savior, right?"

Everyone is surprised at my question, but Dad answers. "Right. We all agree on that."

"Okay. Grandpa, you told me Adam and Eve walked and talked with God, but that ended after they sinned. It's like a barrier is between God and us, right?"

Grandpa looks at me cautiously. "Yeah. That's right."

"So Uncle Jacob, that thick, heavy curtain guarding the most holy place was torn in two. Right?"

"Yeah. That happened in the earthquake."

They're all looking at me, wondering where I'm going with this.

So I tell them what I'm thinking. "What if . . . what if what Jesus did is way bigger than what most people think the Messiah is coming to do? What if Jesus didn't come to save us from our enemies? What if he came to make a way for us to be closer to God?"

They don't agree. They don't disagree. They don't say anything.

I know Jesus came to save us from our sin. The disciples know that too. Dad, Grandpa, and Uncle Jacob know Jesus is the Messiah, but they don't really know he came to save us from our sin.

I feel like I just need to say what I think is happening. It's like holding my nose and jumping into a deep, cold pool of water. I have to just say it. They're all staring at me. It makes me nervous, so I clear my throat . . . and I say it.

"What if Jesus is the absolute, perfect lamb, and he died for our sins?"

Dad is the first to react. "I don't know, son. We need to be careful to follow the Law of Moses."

Grandpa and Uncle Jacob are agreeing with Dad.

So I agree with them too. "Yes, we do. But what if what Jesus just did makes the Law of Moses and everything the prophets said even better? I know it sounds crazy, but think about it. What if that curtain in the temple splitting down the middle meant something? What if it's God's way of saying there are no more barriers between him and us anymore?"

Dad starts to say something, but Grandpa interrupts. "Abe, I think us old people need to start thinking like children."

Jesus said that too!

"What you are suggesting might be right on. But I think we should slow down and wait to hear from the disciples. We don't want to get ahead of ourselves."

But I don't want to quit talking about it. I'm so full of . . . of *something* inside that I feel like I'm going to burst. I'm happy. I'm glad.

I feel so much love . . . I just don't know what all this is I'm feeling. But I do know I have to listen to Grandpa and stop talking about it.

Aunt Sarah comes down the stairs. "Jeremiah is asleep."

Uncle Jacob claps his hands together and stands up. "I think it's time for all of us to go to bed," he says.

I haven't been up long, but I'm happy to go to bed and have all these thoughts to myself. "Good night," I say, and go quietly up the stairs.

I lie in bed, running everything through my head over and over. I get it now! It's all part of God's plan. Jesus was the perfect sacrifice. There's nothing standing between God and us anymore.

I think about that bitter feeling I had when I went to bed last night. It's not here tonight. Tonight, I have hope. I feel like I'm just bursting with hope and so much love for Jesus! I wonder if the world will ever realize what Jesus did. Zag was right to tell me to have faith in God's plan. I put my hand up in the window and give Zag a thumbs-up. I roll over and, with a smile on my face, I fall asleep.

CHAPTER 17

DAY 3—THE TOMB IS EMPTY

When I wake up, it's midmorning, but I feel like I've caught up on all my sleep. I go downstairs and sit at the table.

Aunt Sarah gets up and puts the baby in the cradle. As she walks into the kitchen, she tells me, "I gave some of my secret ingredient to your dad."

"Oh, yum! Thanks!"

Dad grins and nods his head to confirm he has it.

Grandpa asks, "Hey, Abe, how do you feel about going to the temple?"

I think about that, about how it will feel going back there. I would have to relive all the times I saw Jesus there. I'm not sure how I'll feel, but I answer, "Yeah. I think I'd like to do that."

"I think it's a good idea for all of us to go back. It'll help to bring closure to everything we've seen."

Dad holds his hand up. "Count me in."

Uncle Jacob says, "I'm good with that too."

Aunt Sarah puts a bowl of porridge in front of me and says, "Breakfast first!"

Without thinking, I say, "Thanks."

Jeremiah is sitting on Uncle Jacob's lap. They're playing with two small cubes that have different figures carved on each side. They take turns rolling them, trying to get two of the same figures facing up. Jeremiah rolls, throws his arms up, and yells, "I win!"

Aunt Sarah gives him a quick hug. "Wow, Jeremiah! You're good at this game."

He grins at her, then jumps off Uncle Jacob's lap.

I'm still eating when someone knocks on the door.

"I wonder who that could be?" Uncle Jacob asks as he goes to open the door. "Hey, I didn't expect you back so soon. It's Zedekiah! Come on in."

"I have more news," Zedekiah says as he walks in.

Aunt Sarah gives him something hot to drink and he sits down at the table with us.

"So what's the news?" Uncle Jacob asks.

"Are you ready for this?" He has such a big grin on his face we know it has to be good.

We all nod, looking at him expectantly. "The tomb is empty!"

I almost choke on my food, but before I can say anything, Grandpa asks, "What do you mean?"

"The women went there this morning with sweet spices to anoint Jesus's body. When they got there, the stone had been rolled away. And they talked to an angel!"

"What?" We all say it at once.

Zedekiah holds up his hand. "They swear it was an angel. They said he was as bright as lightning."

Grandpa smiles and says, "That's an angel, all right." He's proud to tell us that. "What did he say?"

"He told them Jesus wasn't there, that he had risen. They even looked inside the tomb to make sure, and he wasn't there. They ran back to tell the disciples."

"But—" Uncle Jacob hesitates. "But how do we know someone didn't just take his body?"

We all look at him like, *Why would you say that?*

He holds up his hands in defense. "Sorry. I'm just asking."

Zedekiah nods. "No, you're right. People are going to say that. But Mary Magdalene stayed there. She was kneeling on the ground, and someone asked why she was crying. Want to guess who that was?"

We all wait for him to answer.

He smiles. "It was Jesus."

There's so much excitement inside, I just can't hold it in. I start to cry and laugh at the same time. I swing my legs around to the other side of the bench and give my hands a clap.

Grandpa puts his hands together and, looking up, says, "Thank you, God. Blessed be God forever."

"Jesus told her not to touch him," Zedekiah continues. "Said he hadn't ascended to his Father yet. I'm not sure what that means. Anyway, he told her to go tell the disciples that she had seen him."

We're all excited. I stand up and swing around in a circle on one foot, hitting the air with my hand. "I knew it wasn't over. I just knew it."

Zedekiah grins at me, then warns, "Well, you're going to hear a different story at the temple. The soldiers guarding the tomb knew they'd be in trouble with Pilate, so they went to the chief priests and told them what happened."

Zedekiah shakes his head. "The last thing the chief priests need is for the people to know Jesus is alive. It'll start a movement they won't be able to stop. So they called the elders to figure out what to do."

"Well, what can they do?" Dad says. "They can't stop this."

"They've already paid the soldiers to lie," Zedekiah says. "They even promised to protect them from Pilate. Their story is, the disciples came during the night and took the body when they fell asleep."

Grandpa shakes his head. "Don't they realize Pilate will have them killed for that? The chief priests can't save them from Pilate."

Zedekiah puts a finger up in the air. "Aha! Maybe that's what the chief priests are hoping for. Then there isn't anybody who can dispute their lies."

Uncle Jacob throws up his hands. "Then they win . . . again."

I'm really upset. "It's not right! Jesus changed everything for all of us. The chief priests can't just make it go away with a lie."

Grandpa pats my shoulder and chuckles. "Abe, somehow I think this is all going to work out. What is it you said to us? Have faith in God's plan?"

I come to my senses. Grandpa is right.

Zedekiah tips his cup to finish his drink, then stands to leave. "I'll let you know if I hear anything more. Shalom."

Uncle Jacob thanks him. "Shalom." Then he closes the door behind Zedekiah.

Grandpa gives a loud clap with his hands and rubs them together. "Who's ready to go to the Temple Mount one last time?"

Our moods have changed. This is no longer a sad visit to the Temple Mount but a happy one. Grandpa is leading the way.

We're almost there, but then Grandpa turns right.

"I thought we were going to the Temple Mount?" I ask.

"We are, but I thought we should go see where Jesus spent his last hours. You know, where he was arrested. It's just a small way to honor him."

I'm glad Grandpa thought of that.

We walk down into the Kidron Valley, then up the hill. I forgot what a climb this was. We come to the main road and go left. We walk past the road that would take us to Bethany. I remember Jesus riding that colt. Everybody was so excited to see him.

I wonder if any of those people were in the mob that went to that hill when Jesus was crucified.

We pass the cutoff that would take us to the Golden Gate, then walk just a little farther. Finally, Grandpa says, "The garden of Gethsemane is just to the right here."

I hadn't realized how big the Mount of Olives is. Gethsemane is just a small garden on its lower slope.

As we walk up the hill to the garden, Uncle Jacob explains, "There's no place to have a garden in the city. The wealthy people have private gardens here."

He's right. We walk up the slope on paths of stone. I can see sections of gardens with short fences around them.

Gethsemane has a lot of bushes that offer privacy. There are stone benches carved into the slope along the stone paths. We stop by one and stand there, not saying a word. I imagine Jesus kneeling and praying at one of these benches. I don't want to think about him being arrested here. I want to remember this place as a peaceful, quiet garden where Jesus came to pray.

Grandpa turns to leave, and we follow. We go back down to the main road, then turn right on that cutoff toward the city. We follow the cutoff down the hill into the Kidron Valley, then up again until we reach some steps. We climb several steps until our legs start to hurt. Finally we come onto the Temple Mount through the Golden Gate.

Grandpa says, "Let's go into the temple where we were the other day."

We walk in and sit down on the same bench.

I remember Jesus sitting there with his disciples, watching people drop money into those boxes mounted on the pillars. I remember what Jesus said about that widow. He knew she gave more with her two coins than all the rich people did. I chuckle to myself at how Jesus knew what was in her heart.

Then I correct myself, because Jesus is alive. He *still* knows what's in our hearts. We stay there for a few minutes, watching people drop their coins in the boxes.

Finally, Uncle Jacob gets up and walks toward the temple. "I want to see the curtain that was ripped in half," he says. We follow him and find the curtain has been completely removed. A big wooden barrier now blocks the entrance to the most holy room.

"Isn't that interesting," Grandpa says. "They put a barrier back up."

Nobody says anything. We all just stand there staring at it.

I'd like to see Jesus's tomb, so I ask, "Can we go to those steps on the back side of the temple? I want to look over at that hill. Maybe we'll be able to see the tomb where they put Jesus."

"That's a good idea," Dad says.

So we go out the front of the temple and walk around to the back side of it. We step out on the platform to look out at the tombs . . . but I can't see past those poles on the hill. I shiver at the sight of them.

Suddenly, everything comes back to me, like it's happening all over again. The bitterness is crushing.

Grandpa pulls me out of my thoughts when he points and says, "There it is."

I look over, and I see an open tomb. The stone is rolled over to the side. I make up my mind right there. I don't ever want to fall back into that bitter feeling again. I don't want to think about what *they did* to Jesus. I want to think about what *Jesus did* for us.

Jesus is kind and loving. He wants only good things for everybody. He knew what they were going to do to him, right down to the spitting. But he still did it.

He gave his life for all of us.

I love Jesus so much.

I look over at that tomb and realize it doesn't matter what people think or say. It doesn't matter whether they believe the women or the lies. As far as I'm concerned, Jesus is living, and I can feel that in my heart. I will carry Jesus in my heart for the rest of my life.

We walk back to the Temple Mount and across the courtyard. Grandpa pauses again so we can relive the memories we have of Jesus there.

I think about Jesus throwing the tables over and hollering at the people selling stuff. I start to laugh.

Uncle Jacob hears me and instantly knows what I'm laughing about. "Yeah," he says. "That was great when Jesus turned those tables over. I think that memory will be my favorite."

Dad walks over and gives me a side hug. "You ready to go home, Abe?"

Just hearing Dad say that makes me realize how homesick I am. I miss Mom. I miss my bed. I can't believe it, but I even miss the sheep. "Yes."

"I didn't mean Uncle Jacob's. I mean home."

"I know."

"I'm ready to go home too," Grandpa says.

We step into the tunnel for the last time and make our way to Uncle Jacob's house.

* * *

Our last night at Uncle Jacob's is a happy one. That's amazing, considering all that has happened. We get everything packed so we'll be ready to leave right after breakfast. Then we sit around the fire and talk about Jesus.

"Uncle Jacob," I ask, "will you let us know what happens with Jesus?"

"I promise I will. It's not that long of a walk. I'll be your Zedekiah."

"And we'll make it a point to get back here once in a while," Dad says. "I want to know what happens too."

"I'm really interested in what the disciples will have to say about everything that's happened," Grandpa adds. "I think Abe might be right about it all."

I smile but don't say anything. I'm glad we'll get news about Jesus and the disciples, because I know it's not over.

Grandpa, Dad, and Uncle Jacob relive their experience with Jesus at Bethany. I listen to everything they say as they remind each other of what Jesus taught when they followed him to Perea after he left Bethany.

When the conversation goes back to taxes, I say good night and go upstairs. I change into my bedclothes and crawl into bed. Once I'm there, I can't go to sleep. So I get up on my knees in the bed and rest my arms on the window. I look out at the stars and remember the night I got lost. I looked up at these same stars that night and wished an angel would come to me.

So much is different since that night. I'm different. That adventure for sure changed me, but that isn't the change I'm feeling. There's so much love inside me for Jesus now, sometimes I feel like I'm going to burst. I'm sure it's spilling out to everyone around me.

It reminds me of how much love I felt in the garden of Eden, before Adam and Eve sinned. I realize again how much God wants us to be happy and to love each other. He wants it so much that He came up with a plan to make that happen.

Tears roll down my cheeks. I put my hands together and pray, "Thank you, God, for sending Jesus. Thank you for getting rid of that barrier. Thank you for letting Jesus live in my heart."

Somehow, I know that God can hear what's in my heart. I lie back down in bed. I pull the covers up around my neck and fall asleep.

CHAPTER 18

ABRAHAM'S ADVENTURE IS TOLD

The next morning, we hug and say our goodbyes. We make our way through the streets and come to the gate we first entered. Grandpa has another heated discussion with the officers there. Apparently he wins the argument, because he turns to us with a smile on his face and says, "Time to go."

We walk through the gate and head down the road that leads to home. We get to the bottom of the hill and Grandpa says, "Okay, Abe. Now maybe you can tell me how you knew that lady was Jesus's mother."

My mouth drops open. I know I'm in trouble. I look up at Dad.

He says, "And you can tell me how you knew those two men with that colt were disciples." Dad sees how stressed I am. He laughs and says, "It's okay, son. Sometimes things happen to us in life we can't explain. Things like angels coming to visit in the night."

I look at Dad, shocked to think he might finally believe I went on that adventure. But then Zag did say they would eventually believe me.

Dad puts his hand on my shoulder. "I'm sorry I didn't believe you. But you have to admit—the earth turning, and you going back in time? That's a hard story. It's still hard to believe."

I can tell Dad wants to believe me. But then I remember what Jesus said. Adults have a hard time believing like children do. So I just say, "I know, Dad. It's okay."

Dad laughs. But then he gets quiet. He shakes his head back and forth, still in disbelief. "Abe," he says, "you've been through a lot these last two weeks. I'm proud of how you handled it all." He pauses, then says, "I think it's time we start calling you Abraham."

I can't believe it. He's finally going to call me Abraham!

Grandpa puts his hand on my other shoulder. "Well, it's a long walk home, Abraham. It's time for someone besides me to tell a story. I want to hear all about your adventure."

This is huge. I can't believe it. Not only are they going to call me Abraham, they want to hear about my adventure. They really do believe me!

My head is spinning with excitement. I don't know where to start. I take a deep breath and say, "Wow." The deep breath didn't help to calm my excitement. I take another breath and decide to start at the beginning.

"Well, it all started when you went to find Jesus . . ."

I go on and on, telling them every detail as well as I can remember it. Before we know it, we're making a left turn onto the dirt path that takes us home.

Order Information

REDEMPTION PRESS

To order additional copies of this book, please visit
www.redemption-press.com.
Also available on Amazon.com and BarnesandNoble.com
Or by calling toll free 1-844-2REDEEM.

CPSIA information can be obtained
at www.ICGtesting.com
Printed in the USA
FSHW010106260319

9 781683 147312